MW01146201

The Dawgs Tale

The Story of The Salty Dawg Saloon, The Homer Spit & The Town of Homer, Alaska

DIANE FORD WOOD

 Alaska Press

Anchorage, Alaska

MADE in ALASKA
Permit #3463

COPYRIGHT © 1995 BY DIANE FORD WOOD

PRINTED IN ALASKA
AND THE UNITED STATES OF AMERICA

All rights reserved. No part of this book may be reproduced or transmitted in any form without permission in writing from the publisher.

THE DAWG'S TALE is based primarily on talks with local people; accuracy cannot be guaranteed. Conflicting remembrances are included where known, and readers' comments and clarifications are invited for future editions.

Printed by A.T. Publishing & Printing, Inc.
Anchorage, Alaska
Cover & Book Design by
A.T. Publishing & Diane Ford Wood

❄ *Alaska Press*

P.O. Box 90565
Anchorage, Alaska 99509-0565

DEDICATION

(For being there...)

EDMUND "NED" WOOD

Andie Siobhan Wood
Raquel Wood, Amy Springer, Sylvia Davis
Victor Pantesco, Molly Stonorov

Ned Wood / 1994

4

PREFACE

Posted like silent sentinels all around the town, stand thousands upon thousands of mortal men fixed in ocean reveries...Strange! Nothing will content them but the extremest limit of the land..They must get just as nigh the water as they possibly can without falling in. (From "Moby Dick")

Please, don't call me Ishmael. I am no wanderlusting whale-chaser who swills beer with the best of them. I don't like drinking and I don't work in the fishing industry. In fact, I have no apparent reason to be here. Sometimes I see this reflected in the leathery faces of the fishermen I meet: Sailors who, rounding Pogi after a long day, strain to catch the Dawg's lighthouse beam.

Light's On — Bar's Open
Light's Off — Bar's Closed

Each day, opposites and independents, the well-groomed and the slimed, bow heads to enter, and join each other at the bar. For friends lost, it is a memorial; for friends found, a meeting place. Some spend endless hours here, if only to avoid the cramped quarters of a boat between fisheries. For others, it is the next shot of whiskey, just a stop along the way.

Locals know it as "the Dawg," but the T-shirts and undies stashed behind the bar say: "The Salty Dawg Saloon."

But here I sit, the nearly teetotalling wife of a Quaker man, in the Power Seat if I can swing it, sipping soda, a little too eager for my own good. Maybe it's that bartender Cissy knows I like straws in my drinks and the olive juice left out of my Virgin Marys. Maybe it's the juicy compliments of horny fishermen about my "hellacious blue eyes."

But I doubt it.

Maybe I am just another of Melville's thousands, following any road that leads to water, standing transfixed at its edge.

Visiting the Dawg can be like that, too.

So, stick your head in the door. Ring the bell by the bar. The Dawg is like an old, beached conch shell: If you hold it close, the sea will speak to you. But if you never listen, you'll never hear.

DIANE FORD WOOD

Loree McGee

WHAT'S INSIDE

THE SALTY DAWG SALOON

THE TOWN OF HOMER
& THE HOMER SPIT

APPENDIX

Homer Facts

Homer History

OVERHEARD AT THE DAWG

(From "In Those Days" by the Alaska Pioneers of the
Lower Kenai Peninsula - Used by permission.)

PIONEER QUOTES

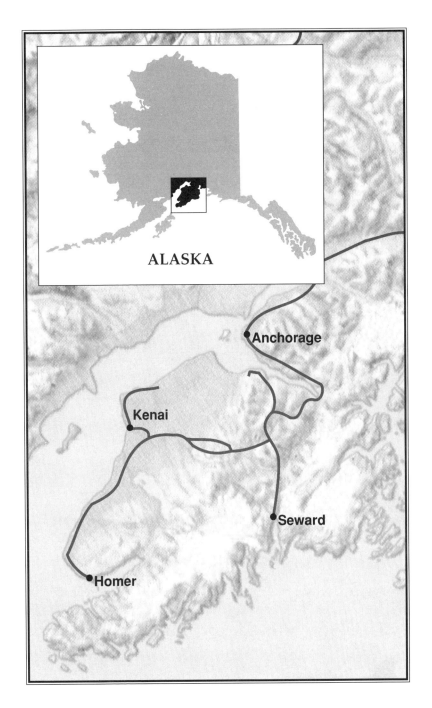

ALASKA

Anchorage

Kenai

Seward

Homer

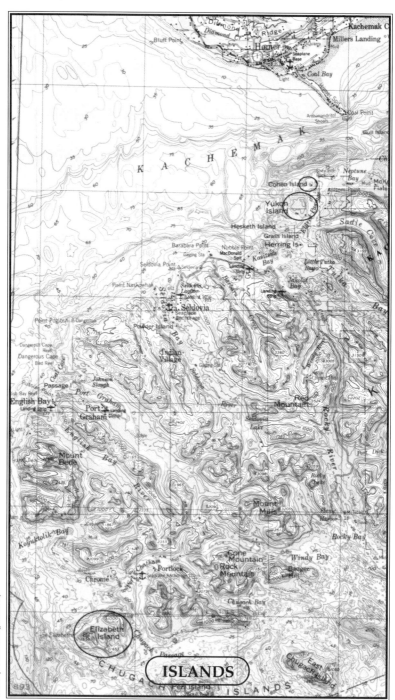

ISLANDS

Courtesy of U.S. Geological Survey

12

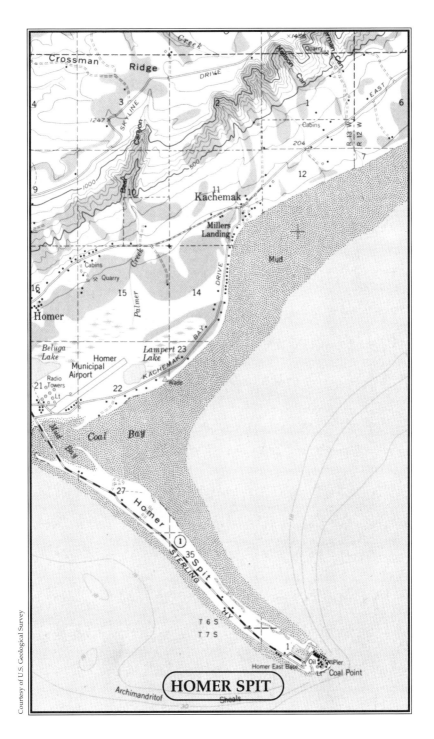

HOMER SPIT

Courtesy of U.S. Geological Survey

13

"...Set in the shadows of the great crystal ice fields, where glaciers calve with whip-cracking fury and humans wander mountainsides with tinkling things to ward off oblivious beasts..." (DFW)

John Child / 1963

INTRODUCTION

From the century's start, the people of Homer survived on the Spit by banding together. Everyone worked to keep the community warm, clean, fed, and entertained. Life was hard, but rewards were great.

Tall grasses towered over children's heads, and horses grazed hungrily on lush Spit pasture lands. Whole neighborhoods played hookey to dig beaches bursting with clams. In the winter, children sledded or skied to school in weather so cold, bedsheets stuck to metal bed frames. Moss and rabbit skins insulated houses, and porcupine stew warmed people's insides.

Families homesteaded, gardened, farmed foxes and fished. Teams of workers built roads and airports, enduring long stretches of unemployment between jobs. Women traveled across the bay to Seldovia to give birth — sometimes confronting waist-high snows to reach the small hospital there. Other new mothers managed alone at home.

Access to the world was by beach and at the whim of the tides. Sometimes, between the erection and natural destruction of docks, bay waters were too rough to land boats. Hardy souls, belongings strapped to their backs, braved the cold green waters of Kachemak Bay to wade ashore.

At post offices, stores, and bars, locals chatted over potbellied stoves, burning coal gathered from area beaches. In lean times, when the post office closed, people rowed skiffs across the bay for mail and supplies. Maneuvering treacherous ice drifts, they gauged helpful tides for Godspeed. At times, the flour and sugar arrived moisture-damaged. And at least once, the boatman didn't make it either.

In community halls and meeting places residents visited, sang, waltzed and foxtrotted. They danced polkas, schottisches, circle two-steps, broom dances and Virginia Reels — often until early morning — while the children slept peacefully nearby.

Near mid-century, with the coming of the roads and a few modern conveniences, some hardships eased. By then, the Spit had been abandoned for the more convenient benchlands. This was before the booms and busts of tourism and commercial fishing — and before the Good Friday Earthquake of 1964.

By 1957, then, everything was quiet on the Homer Spit...

BUT IT GETS HER THERE

There is something inspirational about the old woman who routinely rides her bike past the Salty Dawg Saloon. Head-down determined, she pedals furiously in first gear — never switching to one that might make the trip a little easier.

While she never alters her rhythm or her course, she always gets where she's going — just in her own, individual way.

OVERHEARD AT THE DAWG

The
Salty Dog Saloon

Ned Wood / 1994

Copy of Pirate Painting from the Dawg's Original Location

Chapter 1: *BEGINNINGS*

In a castaway gear shed obtained, appropriately, from a local fisherman, the Salty Dawg Saloon opened on the Homer Spit April 6, 1957. The pub's first owners, Chuck and Phyllis Abbott and Jim

Neely, located the log building by the oil tank farm at the Spit's western tip. Later, it was moved to higher ground.

In the 1950s, opening a bar on the Spit was a radical move. The area was so deserted, many locals found the idea laughable. "Everyone thought it was crazy to put a gear shed out there as a bar," said Wilma Williams, daughter of the fisherman who owned the original building. Chuck Abbott hoped to "make a buck" and increase the value of his oil company property, said Wilma.

When the idea worked, she wasn't surprised: "Chuck was a special guy who was always trying to do something unique." Chuck's wife, Phyllis, agreed: "He was different, that's for sure. He had ideas that wouldn't quit."

For atmosphere, the Abbotts chose a pirate theme to honor "the original salty dawgs." A natural scavenger himself, Chuck scoured Kachemak Bay for jetsam like an old ship's bell, thick portholes, and red and green running lights. He hung them on the bar's walls and ceilings.

"Anytime Chuck would see something, he'd pick it up," said Phyllis. "We did all the decorating, but we never ran the bar." Instead, partner Jim Neely became the first bartender at the Salty Dawg Saloon.

Phyllis Abbott

Chuck and Phyllis Abbott

❅ ❅ ❅

As a practical touch, Chuck hammered a 2-inch firehose to the bar's edge to keep spilled drinks from laps and floors. Local Sam Pratt carved a snake's head and tail for either end of the hose. "Everyone used to joke that it was the only snake in Alaska," said Phyllis. (Alaska has no native snakes.) When the Earthquake of 1964 hit, the makeshift snake floated out on high tide and was lost forever.

Luckily, the Salty Dawg Saloon did not go with it.

A Good Idea

The Dawg was a hit.

Along with atmosphere and location, specials on beer and liquor in the adjacent "Rum Locker" helped attract customers. Phyllis credited manager Ben Walters, Sr. for that success: "People would drive all the way out to the Spit to sample the bargains."

Other customers travelled greater distances: "I don't know how the reputation got around the whole United States. But people, when they came here, just had to go to the Salty Dawg. Our advertising was definitely word of mouth," said Phyllis.

Popular or not, some locals ran heartily away from the Dawg, while others hacked ice to get in to dance, drink and enjoy the fishing village camaraderie.

Ultimately, the Dawg was more of a hobby than a thriving business for the Abbotts, said Phyllis: "We never made a cent out of it until we sold it...but it was a fun time when we had it."

Loree McGee

Changing Hands

In 1960, Earl and Mary Jane Hillstrand, owners of nearby Land's End Resort, bought the Dawg from the Abbotts. The purchase was Earl's idea, according to John and Margaret Mary ("Mo") Hillstrand, the couple's grown children.

"Those two were an incredible team," said Mo. "Dad would get these wild ideas and mother would join him and support him and they would do it together. They were partners in every sense of the term."

The Hillstrands sought out "things that were fun," and the Dawg was a good business venture for them, said Mo: "Dad had a gift for finding opportunities that were unique and also made money." John noted that "Dad liked it because he liked to play cards and sit with the old cronies."

Like the Abbotts, Earl and Mary Jane did not tend bar. Earl was a legislator and Mary Jane was busy with Land's End Resort.

Under the Hillstrands, the atmosphere was "crazy," according to Christ Jacober who bartended for them in 1969. Money abounded, the North Slope was "going great," and the fishing was good. Instead of buying the usual single drink per friend, many people bought rounds in sixes or "six packs," he said.

"It was pretty neat," added John Hillstrand — but he didn't reap the benefits: "You don't drink beer in your dad's bar."

After Earl died in 1974, Mary Jane proclaimed: "I'm not going to be a bar owner." Within months, she put the Dawg up for sale.

Diane Wood/1992

Jane Pascall, Jodean Sauer, Janice Knight and Cissy Rockett

LIVE OR TAPE?

For one patron, a night at the Dawg can mean everything from cleaning bedpans to designing space shuttles. When asked how she is employed, she pulls an "identity du jour" stealthily from the business cards tacked on nearby walls.

"What do you do for a living?" she was asked.

"Oh, I'm a....gynecologist...from...Tucson," she answered.

"I...design couches...for K-Mart," she told another.

OVERHEARD AT THE DAWG

The "Behave Yourself" Years

The next owners, Loree McGee and Bob Sykes, ran the Alaska Railroad food concession from Anchorage to Fairbanks in the early '70s. When the contract ended, Loree toured New Zealand, returned to Alaska, and searched for a new business. In *Alaska Magazine*, she found an ad offering the Dawg for sale. She and Bob investigated, liked what they saw, and bought the bar in 1974.

During Loree and Bob's ownership, time at the Dawg was divided into two seasons: "In the wintertime, this was the fishermen's bar. In the summer, the fishermen kindly stepped aside and let the tourists take over," said Loree.

Loree expected the best from her patrons and they returned in kind. "The fishermen were my protectors. If trouble started, they would gently escort the person outside and tell them not to come back until they could act like gentlemen." In turn, Loree and Bob worked to provide a wholesome atmosphere and staged elegant meals for anyone alone on the holidays.

The ambiance was friendly, but Loree was a stickler on some points: "You couldn't talk real dirty if Loree was standing at the bar," said long-time patron Tim Carr. "It was all business then," agreed Frank Rott, Loree's first customer. "With Loree, you had to behave yourself."

Over time, Loree's affection for the Dawg deepened. It became, she said, "the only place I felt like I belonged." Bob also enjoyed it, but remained in the background, doing repairs and daily inventory, stocking the bar, and changing the sawdust on the floors. As winter approached, Loree painstakingly took everything down from the ceilings and walls to dust: "I hated the job of putting all of those hundreds of cards back up," she said.

After an enjoyable and successful ownership, Loree and Bob stepped aside in 1980. With Bob's failing health and the appearance of "a damn good offer," the Dawg once again changed hands.

Ned Wood / 1994

Sandy Barker and John L. Warren

The Dawg Today

The "damn good offer" came from John Warren, a North Slope oil worker, and his first wife, Gerlene. With John away at the Slope, Gerlene looked for ways to fill her time. Successful in other business ventures, the Dawg looked to her like a fun, worthy investment. She made an offer in 1980 and it was accepted.

Unexpectedly, Gerlene passed away a year later and John was needed to step in at the Dawg. He quit his job on the Slope and moved his two sons, John L. and Randy, to the Spit. Later, he married Lynn Hansen, and together they ran the bar until 1991.

Since then, son John manages the bar, and the family continues to own the Salty Dawg Saloon.

"Both the boys have always been there to help out around the Dawg," said Lynn, "from stocking shelves in the storeroom, to replacing the sawdust on the floors, or putting up Christmas lights on the very tip top of the tower."

❄ ❄ ❄

Sandy Barker, who helps fiance John L. with the bar, looks forward to each season at the Dawg: "It's an exciting time when the Dawg opens — locals coming in to talk about what's been going on all winter, the feeling of one big happy family."

"Closing is a combination of feelings for us — glad that we're going to get a vacation, but also sad to see another season come to an end. So many people come through this little town and bar that have an effect on our lives. The tourists are great to work with and the locals are friends."

At 14 years and climbing, the Warrens have operated the Salty Dawg Saloon longer than any other owners. "We've had offers to sell through the years," said Lynn, "but our gut feelings never let us go through with the deals."

Lynn Warren / 1990

Steven Warren: The Next Generation to Run the Dawg?

The Dawg...A Survivor

For nearly 40 years, the Salty Dawg Saloon has endured the "strange goings-on" of fishing village life. With a history closely aligned to the Great State itself, the Dawg has stood through natural disasters and the Alaska boom/bust economy. Musicians have entertained, traditions have evolved, and fish stories have fooled even the most savvy of customers. But more importantly, thousands of unlikely strangers have connected, conversed, and carved their names in the bar.

In February 1994, the Dawg faced its greatest danger. An intense fire consumed the General Store, the Dawg's closest neighbor. Only by the whim of the winds did the Salty Dawg Saloon — and all that goes with it — survive.

Unlikely Strangers Connecting:
Tina Woodward, Laurie Johnson and Doug "DC" Caldwell

Ned Wood/1994

Main Building

Lynn Warren/1990

*Curtis Cronin, Lynn Warren, John W. Warren
and Ex-Mayor John Calhoun*

Chapter 2: BUILDINGS

"It's hard to believe in 20 years nothing has changed except me." (Patron Tim Carr)

Main Building (Circa 1897)

Step through the Dawg's rustic front door and be surrounded by the oldest surviving structure within the Homer city limits — the main building of the Salty Dawg Saloon. In 1990, Homer High School student Curtis Cronin worked successfully to have this building deemed an official City of Homer landmark.

Lifelong Homerite Tom VanZanten believes that, unlike other old buildings that were torn apart, recycled or moved around, this one was always located on the Spit.

Local historian Janet Klein wrote that it was probably built about 1897, one of the first cabins erected near the time Homer became an official townsite in 1898.

While housecleaning in the 1970s, owner Loree McGee found newspaper insulation in the walls dating back to the late 1800s.

During the coal-seeking days at the turn of the century, the building housed the offices of the Cook Inlet Coal Fields Company from 1899 to 1902. It also served as a grocery store, post office, railroad company office and residence in its time.

In the 1930s, the building prevailed against a slow-moving fire — the first of at least three it would face. Fuelled by coal deposits from the beach, the blaze destroyed nearly every structure on the Spit. Locals paid little mind to the fire: The Spit was nearly deserted and high tides would douse the flames eventually.

In the 1930s and early 1940s, Tom Shelford of Homer and Frank Raby of Seldovia thought the building was a mighty handy place to store tools and fishing gear.

In 1944, Minnie and Alfred Jones, who together ran an early Spit cannery, borrowed the building to live in. They used canvas to partition the single room and driftwood to heat it, according to business partner Florence Jones Elliott.

In the late 1940s, Chuck Abbott bought the shed from Shelford and Raby to use as an office for Standard Oil Company. For a time, said Phyllis Abbott, the building housed at least one oil company employee. After that, Chuck moved it closer to the oil tank farm at the end of the Spit. There, it would become the Salty Dawg Saloon.

For construction enthusiasts (who can decipher the language), Janet Klein describes the building as made of "round log members, butted and spiked into vertical quarter-sawn logs...Fascia members and exposed rafters are round and the gable ends are sheathed with small-diameter vertical round logs."

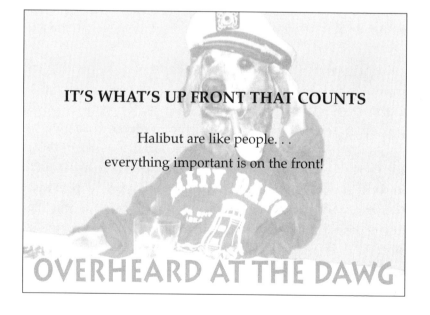

IT'S WHAT'S UP FRONT THAT COUNTS

Halibut are like people. . .
everything important is on the front!

OVERHEARD AT THE DAWG

Adjoining Room (Circa 1909):

Housing the piano, long carved benches, and the ever ready jukebox and television, the adjoining room connects to the main building by a small addition.

In 1909, it was erected as a barn on the Woodard Homestead about where Pioneer Avenue meets the Bypass Road. (James Woodard, an early Homer settler, was a boatman lost while returning from a rowing trip across the bay. As legend has it, loaded down with mail and supplies, he was asked to carry a dog sled back to Homer. His skiff was full, but he finally agreed. After setting sail, he was never seen again.)

In the late 1950s, Homer resident Leo Rollins trucked the Woodard barn to the Spit where it was used to enlarge the Salty Dawg Saloon.

According to Janet Klein, this room was used, at other locations, as an early schoolhouse, post office, grocery store and private home. Made of 12-inch logs with dovetail notching, it sports an existing door with "fanciful heavy strap hinges" and a porthole window that may have been added later, she noted.

Ned Wood/1994

The Adjoining Room

33

Ned Wood/1994

The Tower/Lighthouse

Tower/Pool Room/Lighthouse (1964):

"Its the room with the view and music to soothe your soul — However, sometimes it's not so soothing!" (Owner Lynn Warren)

The newest, and most famous of the Dawg's buildings — the landmark tower — is also the tallest structure on the Spit.

Designed and built by Earl Hillstrand, it was added to the Dawg after the Earthquake of 1964 to enclose a water tank. "Earl always liked lighthouses," widow Mary Jane Hillstrand told the *Anchorage Times.*

Although the tower was never a true lighthouse (the light is turned off when the bar closes), it is marked on marine charts. This makes the Dawg's tower a true nautical landmark. (See NOAA story, Chapter 6.)

These days, the tower's first floor houses the bar's pool-room; the second, John L.'s hobby room; the third and fourth, an apartment; and the top floor, the beacon light. John L. resided there during his last two years of high school, and now the tower is left vacant for the convenience of the family.

Lynn Warren/1993

Staying the Night in the Tower: Steven and Sammy Warren

Cissy Rockett

Garrett Myers at Play in the Poolroom

A great source of afternoon sun, the tower "creaks, leaks and sways in the wind," said Lynn. "The sounds from the poolroom and the rest of the bar drift up, but for visiting friends and family, it's all part of the Alaskan excitement. We've had many opportunities to rent it out, but we never chose to do it."

In its original state, the tower housed a large 5,000 gallon storage tank that supplied the Dawg with water. According to John Hillstrand, it was dismantled on Ohlson Mountain and brought to the Dawg in numbered pieces: "It was one of those old wooden water tanks put together like an old whiskey barrel."

Frank Rott remembered when running water came to the Spit and the tank was no longer needed: "I'm the guy who tore it down. It took about four days with help from the Hillstrand kids — we had to save every piece." Later, when those pieces disappeared, John Hillstrand found some of them built into a friend's wall — but he won't say whose.

Salty Pup Cafe/Storeroom (Prior to 1927)

Photographs show a petite log shanty called "The Salty Pup Cafe" resting behind the Dawg in the pub's first days. The name is another example of the Abbott's penchant for titles with "salty" in them. (See SALTY DUCK photos, pp. 20 and 42.)

Currently used as a storeroom, no one seems to remember the Salty Pup as an up and running restaurant. At least two old-timers recalled buying hot bowls of chili at a "little place at the end of the Spit" in the late '50s, but they weren't sure where it was.

Phyllis Abbott felt the Pup must have been a short-lived business — she doesn't remember much about it either. A relative, Alice Abbott, ran a seafood restaurant then, she said, but it was in a different location on the Spit.

Salty Pup Cafe/Storeroom

37

Prior to 1927, the little building was used as a post office on Beluga Slough. After the Earthquake of 1964, when owner Earl Hillstrand moved the Dawg by the boat harbor, the Pup was also moved. Enlisted as a private storeroom, it stands at the Dawg's right side.

Janet Klein noted that the building's logs have "square and saddle-notched corners and planks cover(ing) the gable ends." Several logs show evidence of shipworm damage, she said, hinting that they may have been immersed in saltwater for a long period of time.

The Salty Pup in Winter

Rum Locker (Prior to 1964)

"It's not the alcohol that gives a bar its atmosphere and reputation, but the people who run and frequent it." (DFW)

Possibly the Spit's first true liquor store, the Rum Locker is no longer part of the Salty Dawg Saloon. A shack the size of a small room, it sat behind the Dawg in its earliest days. Manager Ben Walters, Sr. ran such great bargains out there, said Phyllis Abbott, it helped attract customers to the Spit.

After the Earthquake of 1964, the Rum Locker was relocated between the Salty Pup storeroom and Silver Fox Charters. Guarded by an old padlock, the Hillstrands used it to store liquor.

Old photographs show the Rum Locker's sign as similar to the Dawg's, and the building itself was "just as ratty as the Dawg," noted Mo Hillstrand.

In the 1960s, the Dawg faced a second trial by fire when the Rum Locker burned down just a few feet away. Possibly because the buildings did not share a foundation, once again, the Dawg and its famous tower remained unscathed.

The Dawg in Its Original Location

Phyllis Abbott

Chuck Abbott

Chapter 3: 🇫ACES 🇧EHIN🇩 🇹HE 🇧A🇷

Owners & Operators

1957-1960

Charles B. "Chuck" Abbott
Phyllis Abbott
Jim Neely

The original owners of the Salty Dawg Saloon — Charles B. "Chuck" Abbott, Phyllis Abbott and Jim Neely — started with no more than an old log cabin, a few dollars, and a lot of inge-nuity. Thirty-eight years later, Phyllis still lives in Homer and the Dawg is going strong, too.

CHARLES B. "CHUCK" ABBOTT

The man who thought up "The Salty Dawg Saloon," Chuck Abbott, was born July 18, 1916 in Prineville, Oregon. When Pearl Harbor was bombed, he was Alaska-bound via the Gulf, heading for Anchorage and a job with the Corps of Engineers. As a draftsman for the Corps, he created a famous map of Alaska superimposed over the lower 48.

In 1950, he journeyed to Homer with his first wife and became a wholesale distributor for Standard Oil Company. In 1954, his wife died, and three years later, he opened the Salty Dawg Saloon with his new wife, Phyllis.

Following the sale of the Dawg in 1960 to the Hillstrands, Chuck became active in civic affairs by mapping and lettering. In 1962, he suffered his first stroke, and on January 26, 1966, he died in Anchorage.

Buried on the Abbott property in Homer, Chuck Abbott left behind Phyllis, daughters Lynette, Charlene, Jane and Ann, and stepson Phillip Brudie.

PHYLLIS ABBOTT

On New Year's Eve 1956, Bill Abbott arranged a blind date for brother Chuck in California. After corresponding for six months, the matchmaking of Chuck and Phyllis blossomed.

"Chuck was a good dancer...and a marvelous map draftsman," said Phyllis. "I came up here for a vacation and never left."

Phyllis was born in Compton, California, in the days when "boundless acres" existed for children to play in.

By 1957, she was a new Alaskan, and looking back, she described herself as "very naive, very good natured." Pioneer life taught her a few life lessons, she said: "I've learned to fight since."

A third generation Californian, Phyllis believes the trailblazing spirit of her grandparents helped prepare her for bush life. (Her grandparents traveled overland by covered wagon to the West.) "If my grandparents could do that, I could, too."

John Child / 1959

SALTY DUCK on Parade

Phyllis Abbott

The Abbott's Fifth Wedding Anniversary at the Dawg

On June 14, 1957, the couple homesteaded Cohen Island on the southern shore of Kachemak Bay, not far from Homer. Named after a turn-of-the century Inlet trader, the island is heavily wooded with spruce trees. Chuck built a cabin on the beach and, together, the Abbotts cultivated the land and "proved up" on August 18, 1958.

"It was the highlight of my life," said Phyllis, who particularly savored the moments when people stopped by in boats for coffee. For transportation to and from the mainland, the Abbotts used a two-seater amphibious vehicle called the SALTY DUCK. The boat/truck moved freely on land and in water. Later, they replaced it with the TIN CUP, a similar vehicle.

Phyllis now lives on the mainland and she and her grown children still enjoy Cohen Island today.

After Chuck and Phyllis were married five years, friends threw a surprise anniversary party for them at the Salty Dawg Saloon. That was the last time Phyllis Abbott visited the bar.

John Child / 1956

Jim Neely

JIM NEELY

Because the Abbotts preferred not to run the bar, partner Jim Neely became the first official bartender of the Salty Dawg Saloon. A "congenial person, well-liked in town," according to Phyllis, Jim joined the venture because he liked the novelty of working on the Spit.

Old-timer Wilma Williams thought of Jim as a "really fun person, a fantastic guitarist, a wonderful bartender, and a good b.s.'er."

After years of living lively, Jim burned out, she said, and became a minister. He died a few years later.

John Child/1956

"Whiskerinos" — Jim Neely (Center)

45

Mo Hillstrand

Earl Hillstrand

Mo Hillstrand

Mary Jane Hillstrand

1960-1974

Earl D. Hillstrand
Mary Jane Hillstrand

1942, Washington, DC:

"Mary Jane, we're going to Anchorage."

"Where's that?" she replied.

The second owners of the Salty Dawg Saloon, Earl and Mary Jane Hillstrand came to Alaska in the '40s and lived in a Quonset hut. Despite Mary Jane's formal upbringing, "She took risks with Dad," said daughter Mo. "They had a lot of fun together."

Both Hillstrands grew up in Tacoma, Washington. Earl was born August 20, 1913; and Mary Jane, January 17, 1914. In 1935, they married, and had four children: Gail, Mary Joanne, John Wesley and Mary Margaret.

EARL HILLSTRAND

A lawyer and a legislator, Earl Hillstrand was educated at the College of Puget Sound and George Washington University. After coming to Alaska, the couple homesteaded on Lake Otis Road in Anchorage.

Mo called her father "visionary, strong, honest" and "a statesman rather than a politician." The way she saw it, "Dad was a dreamer who made things happen...He let you know where he stood — and he stood by what he believed in.

"Dad was a pretty nice guy," added son John Hillstrand.

John Child / 1984

Land's End Resort

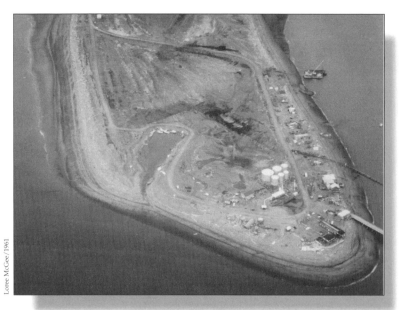

Loree McGee / 1961

End of Spit - 1961

In his time, Earl wore many hats: He was active in Alaska real estate and as an attorney. In 1972, he was re-elected to his seventh term in the Alaska legislature. His pet projects included the capital move, the Alaska Permanent Fund program, and the Alaska Native Claims Settlement Act. He also sold insurance, and on occasion, fished commercially with Clem "Red" Tillion.

In 1960, the Hillstrands bought the Salty Dawg Saloon from the Abbotts — two years after building Land's End Resort at the end of the Homer Spit. Although the Hillstrands did not tend bar at the Dawg, Earl took care of the ordering, bookkeeping and paperwork with Mary Jane's help.

MARY JANE HILLSTRAND

John Hillstrand thought of mom, Mary Jane Hillstrand, as "very nice, prim and proper, Mary Jane." In the family's early days, she covered the entire yard with her gardening, he said: "We had a homestead and she had a garden we all ate off of."

The word "lady" also came to daughter Mo's lips — probably because of Mary Jane's finishing-school education. A voracious reader, Mrs. Hillstrand "lived for fun," played violin, won prizes for photography, and did charcoal drawings in the early days. "She had a creative flair," said Mo.

Earl and Mary Jane Hillstrand ran the Dawg until Earl's death from pancreatic cancer on January 22, 1974. Mary Jane passed away from emphysema on February 5, 1980.

Loree McGee

Bob & Loree's First Christmas Tree at the Dawg

1974-1980

⊢•→◦→•⊣

Loree McGee
Robert "Bob" Sykes

"The friendship of those we serve is the foundation of our progress." (From a Christmas card sent by Bob and Loree to patrons.)

The Dawg's third owners, Loree McGee and Robert "Bob" Sykes, held the Alaska Railroad dining concession from Anchorage to Fairbanks before buying the Dawg in 1974. A good team, according to friend Christ Jacober, "They enjoyed each other — just business partners." They were the third owners of the Salty Dawg Saloon.

In 1984, Bob passed on, and Loree, now 78, lives in Oklahoma. Through the years, she worked mostly in the dining and bar business. "It's the only thing I know," she told the *Anchorage Times* in 1978.

Loree maintains a collection of correspondence and postcards from all over the world.

Bob Sykes and Loree McGee

51

Loree McGee

Loree McGee

Loree McGee

LOREE MCGEE

Born in Sunset, Texas, Loree grew up in Lawton, Oklahoma. She came to Alaska after living for 17 years in Miami, Florida. "I wanted to see some more of this world and I worked my way up here," she said. "I stopped off a year in Las Vegas, but when I saw Homer, I knew that was it."

While living in the "Halibut Capital of the World" (Homer), Loree's fishing days were cut short. On her last expedition, she "inadvertently" hooked a fish so big, it took four men to harpoon and get it in the boat.

After viewing pictures of the 150-pound fish, Loree thought: "Poor creature — he fought the battle of survival all of those years and I had to catch him." After that, she sold her rod and reel and never went fishing again.

While she owned the Dawg, Loree built the second floor over Silver Fox Charters for living quarters.

Loree McGee/1980

Loree McGee

53

Loree McGee

Bob Sykes

ROBERT "BOB" SYKES

Born in New Bedford, Massachusetts, Bob Sykes was 6′2″, 200 pounds, and very slim and trim, according to Loree. "He was my partner and friend."

Although Bob refused to work behind the bar, Loree figures he liked being at the Dawg because he never returned to the construction trade. He did, however, work on improvements to the buildings. He erected a ceiling and floor in the pool room, and connected the Salty Pup storeroom to the main building with the help of friend Earl Kramer.

After Bob and Loree sold the bar to the Warrens in 1980, Bob returned to Massachusetts to be with his mother and sister. There, he died of cancer of the esophagus in 1984.

"Bob got along with everybody," said Loree. "He was very friendly, but kind of bashful — but when he did make a friend, he kept 'em."

Bob Sykes Playing Pool

Lynn Warren/1982

John W. Warren and Lynn Warren

1980-Present

Gerlene Warren
John W. Warren
Lynn Warren

"The Salty Dawg Saloon has been good to us. We are not looking to own another bar. It is so unique, we could not find another one to take its place." (Lynn Warren)

A year after John and Gerlene Warren became the fourth and current owners of the Salty Dawg Saloon, Gerlene died unexpectedly. Quitting his oil company job, John moved his two sons, John L. and Randy, from the Homer hills to the Spit. It would make it easier, he decided, to juggle being a single dad with running the Dawg.

In 1982, John married Lynn Hansen in the little log Catholic Church in Homer. Together they ran the bar, took care of the family, and fished on their boat the CAPE KASILOF.

JOHN W. WARREN

Born in Cotulla, Texas, John grew up in New Mexico. He and Gerlene (born in Willard, New Mexico) moved to Alaska to work in 1969. After living in Fairbanks, Kenai, and Wasilla, the family moved to Homer in 1979. John drove semi-trucks, built and sold houses, and worked for 12 years for ARCO on the North Slope of Alaska.

Lynn Warren / 1981

Lynn Warren

LYNN WARREN

Born to an Air Force family, Lynn's birthplace was Cocoa Beach, Florida. She traveled the USA and Europe with her family.

In 1978, she moved to Alaska from Minnesota. Her mother, Pat Hansen, went along for the ride. In Anchorage, Lynn worked as a dental assistant at the Teamster Dental Clinic.

After spending several weekends in Homer, she learned of a job opening there. Two weeks later, she was a Homerite working for Jim Meesis, DDS. Three years later, she met John Warren and the Salty Dawg Saloon became part of her life.

In the late 1980s, when son John L. Warren worked for an Anchorage distributing company, John and Lynn asked if he'd like to manage the Dawg. "For one reason or another, he wasn't into it," said Lynn. Years passed, and in February 1991, John L. reconsidered — he was ready to make the change.

"Well, the wheels started turning," said Lynn, and by April 1991, John L., his fiancee, Sandy Barker, and Sandy's son Brian, all moved to Homer.

"We led John through the operation, and by July 12, 1991, we were headed down the Alcan with a puppy, a kitty, and all our belongings in a horse trailer. We were moving to New Mexico to get on with the next chapter in our lives."

Lynn Warren

Gerlene Warren and John L. Warren

Lynn Warren / 1984

John L. Warren and Randy Warren

With John L. managing the Dawg, John and Lynn feel comfortable: "It sure has relieved us of a lot of worry having John L. do such a good job. For now, we're only a phone call away, and we come up every year to take care of some legal paperwork and visit with friends and family."

These days, John and Lynn raise livestock and horses on 18 acres. "The Dawg still carries on in New Mexico for us," said Lynn. "We have a thoroughbred racehorse named 'Salty Dog Sis' — her win pictures hang in the bar." They also continue to wear their Salty Dawg hats and shirts: "Strangers see us wearing them and they've either been to our place or know someone who has. It's really a small, small world."

Happy New Year: Lynn and John W. Warren

Diane Svymbersky

Bartenders & Employees
(A Random List)

Long-time Dawg patrons remember bartenders and workers with names like Angel, Lana, Holly, Pat, Coral, Patti, Ruby Star and Sherri — but a formal list was never kept.

➣ The Fifties ➣

Jim Neely

The first bartender at the Dawg, Jim was part-owner along with Chuck & Phyllis Abbott until they bought him out.

Ben Walters, Sr.

Ben managed the bar and Rum Locker for the Abbotts and replaced Jim Neely as bartender at the Dawg's original location. "He did a good job for us out there. Ben was a great guy. He read a lot on his own, and would have liked to become a lawyer," said Phyllis Abbott.

Name Forgotten

"This guy had been all over the world and always wore a cap with a bill on it. He tended bar in the Philippines," said Wilma Williams.

≈ The Sixties ≈

Willie Flyum

Willie worked the bar in the late '60s and, according to Frank Rott, "Willie did some wild things in those days." John Hillstrand called Willie: "a character — best bartender dad ever had."

Christ Jacober

Pronounced "Chris," Christ retired from the Army in 1960, journeyed to Alaska, and tended bar for a short time for the Hillstrands. He and his wife Maxine also owned the Totem Drive-in, now called "Addie's."

"Christ was the kind of person you'd go to as a confidant," said Mo Hillstrand.

Dick Little

Dick watched the bar for several years under the Hillstrands. Frank Rott recalled how Dick dressed elegantly in silk shirts: "People walked in, saw him, and walked out. When he tended bar, it was like walking into a church."

John Hillstrand thought differently: "On a good night, Dick looked like a pirate with a bloody knife in his teeth." John's sister Mo remembered Dick as "a really cheerful guy. He'd listen patiently to people's stories."

Doug & Louise Young

"Great bartenders," according to John Hillstrand, the couple worked for the Hillstrands for three years. "Everybody loved them in town...they were lovely people," said John. Mo described Louise as "gregarious" and remembered her "raucous laugh."

⋙ The Seventies ⋙

Pauline Bonvillian

Loree McGee's sister, Pauline, lived in Florida and took two long vacations in Alaska. "When the night bartender finished their shift, we would go over to close up," said Loree. "She really enjoyed it."

Alex Chapple

Loree McGee's favorite employee, Alex Chapple, still lives and works in Homer.

Alex Chapple

≈ *The Eighties & Nineties* ≈

Sandy Barker

"What am I doing here?" Sandy asked during her first Alaskan winter in 1984. After weathering the season, she and son Brian planned on being lifelong Alaskans.

Before moving to Homer, Sandy was a department manager with an Anchorage food chain. She is engaged to John L. Warren.

Sandy Barker / 1993

John L. Warren and Sandy Barker

Birdie

Hired by the Warrens in 1988, Birdie has bartended for about seven years. Known for her excellent baking abilities, she is especially good at wedding cakes.

Diane Desmond

A skier who sometimes works in Colorado, Diane cannot be pinned down for very long.

"Jerri Lynn"

Diane Svymbersky described Jerri Lynn as "A bartender so beautiful, every guy fell in love with her."

Alan Kelly

Known as "a nice guy" and "a world-class conversationalist," Kelly has bartended at Down East Saloon and fishes commercially.

Kevin Murphy

Kevin is an educated fisherman somehow connected to a famous artist. He is also known as "somewhat of a ladies' man," according to Diane Svymbersky.

Lynn Warren/1989

Lynn Warren/1985

Jerri Lynn   *Trevor, Kevin Murphy and George*

Cissy Rockett

A bartender for 13 years at the Dawg, Cissy was hired by the Warrens in 1982. Originally, she came to Alaska to visit a home-town (California) friend and, like many before her, never left.

A charter member of the Spit Rat Club, Cissy is famous for finding the most valuables in the sawdust.

Cissy grows beautiful window box flowers, is great with crafts, and is a killer Scrabble player. She has also placed as a driver in hot rod races at the Homer Winter Carnival.

The wife of Chuck, a steel man, she is mom to Garrett and Chance.

Cissy Rockett

Garrett Myers

Chance Rockett

Susan Snow

Hired recently by the Warrens, Susan is a hard worker with a pleasant smile.

Diane Svymbersky

In 1980, Diane Svymbersky applied for a job at Land's End Resort. While waiting to hear, she spent time at the Dawg and learned that bar help was needed there. Gerlene Warren hired her, and Diane never went back to Land's End.

After 14 years at the Dawg, she said: "It's fun; I love it." She likes to watch the patrons change with the seasons — more locals in winter, tourists in the summer.

Her maiden name initials — "DB" — (Diane Baley) are carved in the bar.

Diane is mom to Tobey Baley and Michael Svymbersky, and the wife of Joe Svymbersky, a North Country Charters boat captain.

Diane Svymbersky

Dave VanZanten

A fisherman, Dave is noted for his "sharp, dry wit and good sense of humor," according to Diane Svymbersky.

A "Names Only" List

Mary VanZanten, Peggy B., Jane, George, Kerry, Shelly, Dorothy, Joe Cavo, Tina, Colleen, Terry, Alma, Greg, Pauline, Laurie Johnson, Linda and Karin.

Loree McGee

Frank Rott

Chapter 4: *PARTICULAR PATRONS*

Over the years, the Dawg has seen many infamous locals, famous patrons and curious canines. But one man, Frank Rott, seemed to personify the spirit of the Salty Dawg Saloon. Before his death on May 15, 1994, Frank lived on the Spit for 27 years.

FRANK JOHN ROTT
(1907-1994)

"I don't mingle with the old people. That's right, only with young people. There are a lot of things they do, I know, that's wrong, but I accept it." (Frank Rott, 1977 Interview with Steve Kline)

My interview with the late Frank Rott, one of the Homer Spit's most infamous residents, took place on his porch over July 4, 1993.

Tall and lanky at 86, Frank was cranky with me like an old movie star. Outright, he told me I had "rocks in my head" to suggest such high-season timing for an interview. Committed to keeping an eagle eye on "Frank's Parking" (which stretched before us on the Spit), he seemed like a distracted old man of the sea.

Diane Szymbersky

Frank Rott

Other than his grumpy behavior, Frank seemed pleased to contribute to this book. And with his death less than a year later, I was glad to have endured the eccentric moments.

Popular with the locals, Frank inspired a lot of attention in his time. At the Dawg, he was named president of the Spit Rat Club, was assigned a special price for drinks ($1), and for more than a decade, the bar opened every year on his birthday (February 26th).

In Frank's obituary in the *Homer Tribune*, correspondent Randi Somers listed his many nicknames:

Hunk

Smiling Hunk

King of the Spit Rats

Governor of the Spit

— and Grandpa

I asked Frank about the Hillstrands, his close friends and mentors for nearly 30 years. Frank's apartment was built for his use by John and Nancy Hillstrand near their Spit business, Coal Point Trading Company.

Frank said the relationship began in 1967 — the year he left Green Bay, Wisconsin, after 42 years on the railroad. He came to Alaska, he said, because he liked to fish and had a son living in Soldotna. After arriving in Homer, Frank cut firewood, unasked, for Earl Hillstrand on the Spit. Impressed, Earl invited Frank to camp on his property and things developed from there.

Frank's friends pointed to Frank's usefulness:

"In the winter, Frank kept the water running at Land's End," said Diane Svymbersky. "I'm sure Frank was just totally dependable — because he expected that of everybody else." Diane also suspected Frank's popularity was because "He was always like everybody's grandpa." Frank held big crab parties at his place, and at the Dawg's annual Thanksgiving dinner, Frank cooked a turkey and brought beans.

Christ Jacober, who bartended at both the Salty Dawg Saloon and Land's End Resort, said: "Frank did everything for the Hillstrands. They could rely on him, especially in the wintertime when they were closed up." This included cutting wood, plumbing, and performing general repairs and cleanup.

While Earl and Mary Jane Hillstrand have passed away, I asked daughter Mo about Frank: "He was eccentric, but I loved him as a human being," she said. His popularity on the Spit, she thought, had something to do with his infamy: "A legend had built up around him."

Ned Wood / 1994

❋ ❋ ❋

While Frank had not visited the Dawg much in his final years, Lynn Warren often dropped by to bring his mail, and — when they were on sale — bananas. "He loved hearing what was happening in the Dawg...and he would tell me all the latest goings-on in his neighborhood."

After the Warrens moved away, they phoned him occasionally and Frank would make informal football bets with John. "He loved his Green Bay Packers."

❋ ❋ ❋

When Frank died on May 15, 1994, his ashes were scattered from Coal Point to Sadie Cove by friends. A memorial wreath hangs in the Dawg in his honor. "It's our lifeline to him," said Lynn.

Whatever the source of his popularity, it seems that Frank's usefulness, his ability to accept the idiosyncrasies of the young and to contribute to their lives, were key to the friendships he developed over the years.

Christ Jacober noted: "Frank was a great all-around guy. I was sure sorry when I heard he passed away."

Nancy Hillstrand told the *Homer Tribune*: "He (Frank) would want us to celebrate and smile — that was his motto of life."

❋ ❋ ❋

A TRUE STORY

Just before I left small town New Hampshire for Alaska, one of my neighbors said: "Say hello to John Jacobson (not his real name) when you get there."

I had never met the man.

"Alaska is a big state," I said, being tactful. "But I sure will if I see him."

One week after landing in Homer, I walked toward the old Porpoise Room restaurant on Fish Dock Road. A drunk staggered up beside me, offering to sell me something in a heavy New England accent.

I couldn't resist asking.

"By any chance — Is that a New Hampshire accent?"

"Yes, indeed, ma'am. My name is John Henry Jacobson from Jaffrey, New Hampshire — Glad to make your acquaintance!"

(And yes, I said hello for my neighbor.)

OVERHEARD AT THE DAWG

FAMOUS CUSTOMERS

In general, Alaskans don't fuss much about celebrity or financial status. While the Dawg does have its share of infamous locals — the Warren Beattys of the fishing industry — most would not take kindly to being mentioned here.

Rumor has it that Walter Cronkite stopped by, and Morton Dean came in with a CBS crew. Former Alaska Governor Jay Hammond visited, as did actor Earnest Borgnine, actor/director Steven Seagal, and his ex-wife actress Kelly LeBrock.

Cissy Rockett remembered Kevin McHale visiting — a 6'10" star basketball player from the University of Minnesota and Boston Celtics: "You can't imagine how far he had to duck just to get in the front door. It was too funny."

❄ ❄ ❄

Lynn Warren remembered another famous encounter, also of the athletic kind:

In town for the "Jimmy Huega Express" benefit for Muscular Dystrophy, top skier Jean-Claude Killy purchased a hot pink T-shirt at the bar. (In the 1980s, most men weren't wearing pink.) When Jean-Claude bought one, she was thrilled:

"You see, John," she said to her husband (who was sure the pink tees wouldn't sell), "Jean-Claude Killy likes them — and he'll look damn good in it!"

"Killy was wonderful," said Lynn.

❄ ❄ ❄

Diane Svymbersky

Tobey Baley and "Dittyboo Dog"

TAKING YOUR DOG TO THE DAWG

Yes, Virginia, there is no Salty Dawg.

Some people think the famous photo of the dog with the pipe is THE DAWG. The truth is, there is no real Salty Dawg. The photos were staged by a California couple for fun, and the name of the bar refers to pirates. Many memorable bow wows, however, have spent time kicking sawdust, doing tricks, and just plain hanging out at the Salty Dawg Saloon.

"Everyone used to take their dogs to the Dawg," said Frank Rott, and many strays have found new homes there.

Bartender Diane Svymbersky found puppy "Dittyboo Dog" one day at work. Not interested in tricks, Ditty spent most of her time sleeping at Diane's feet. "People always thought she was THE dog," said Diane.

Unlike Dittyboo, "Max" was a trickster's delight. Small, black, and short-haired, his antics cost owner Fred Bannick money. Max's best trick was ringing the bell by the bar. This meant that Fred (or the person who put Max up to it) would have to buy drinks for everyone. "Max would jump up on the counter and really have a ball pulling that rope," said Loree McGee.

Loree's dogs "Candy" and "PB" were also well-known at the Dawg. PB, a little white poodle, was especially noted for his musical talents: "One day, Alex (an employee) was sitting at the bar holding PB on her lap while a Barbara Streisand record was playing on the music box. All of a sudden, PB threw his head back, and started to yell along with the record. And so, I say my PB sang with Barbra Streisand."

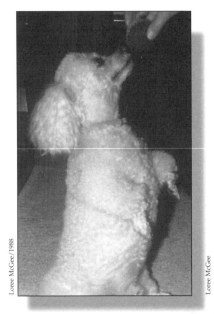

Loree McGee/1988

Loree McGee

"PB"

Loree McGee

"Candy" — A Gift from a NOAA Boat

Another Dog at the Dawg (Note Spit Rat Club Jacket)

"Max" Ringing the Bell

John Child/1964

Dog with Master - 1964

These days "Bud," an 8-year-old golden retriever mix, is the resident dog. Owned by Manager John L. Warren, Bud does tricks — but not for everyone.

"Bud picks out his own people, lures them outside, and prompts them to throw sticks in the parking lot," said Sandy Barker.

"Bud"

For some dogs, the Salty Dawg Saloon has been a final memory. Kendall Koepecke's black lab (memorialized in a framed picture near the main door), was flattened by a car just outside.

In 1976, Frank Rott's dog, Oscar, a black lab/setter, also lost his life nearby. After running on the beach with some children, Oscar followed them across the road. Hit by a car, Oscar managed to crawl a few more feet, and fell dead at the Dawg's front door. "It was such a devastating thing to Frank," said Loree, "that after that, Frank only had cats."

But the cats gave Frank great pleasure, said Lynn Warren: "Frank would laugh and say he was the only man on the Spit with his own cat house!"

Lynn Warren / 1990

"Kobuk"

Lynn Warren / 1983

"Lotus"

A few cats, too, have found their way to the Dawg:

"Lotus," a feline owned by John and Lynn Warren, did well contending with Spit life: "She kept a careful eye on all the other critters she didn't want to deal with — eagles and owls in winter; seagulls and crows in summer; and the dogs and stray cats that wanted to take over her territory," said Lynn. "When the bar closed, she'd go down with us and check it all out."

"Kobuk," John and Lynn's next cat, liked to visit bartender Cissy and play pool after hours. "Yep, he'd get up on the table and bat the balls around," said Lynn. After all the balls were in the pockets, Lynn and John would bring them out and the game would start again.

And finally — befitting the Dawg's pirate theme — a colorful parrot visited in the 1980s. Inside the bar, the beautiful bird moved from one shoulder to the next. Outside, he sat on the rusty anchor and stopped traffic as drivers caught sight of him.

John W. Warren

Carl Jones

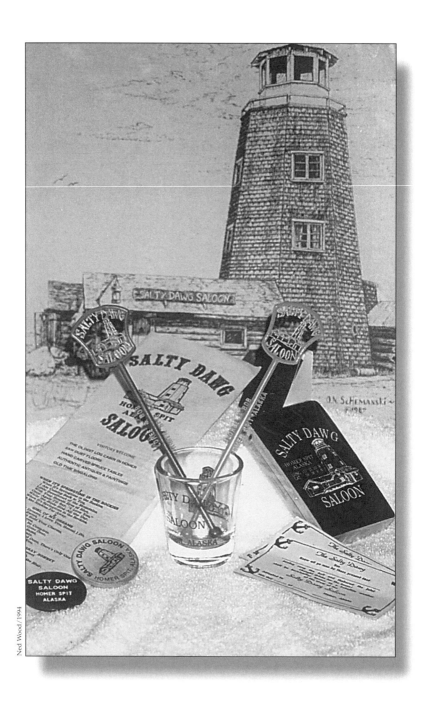

Ned Wood / 1994

Chapter 5: *TRADITIONS*

From the Dawg's earliest days, traditions have evolved and become an important part of the routine.

Carving

Tim Carr, long-time patron, remembered drunken fishermen with gauze-wrapped fingers trying to carve on the bar with jackknives folding in on their fingers.

In the mid-1980s, when a deckhand from Seward attempted to use a bait chopper on the bar, owner John W. Warren called carving quits forever.

Drinks & Libations

Originally, all drink orders yielded a beer, said Frank Rott, mostly because there was little demand for hard liquor. "Ask for any kind of beer you wanted and they'd give you a bottle of Rainier — like it or not. And they sold a lot of it, ho-ho!"

In Loree's day, she said: "We didn't serve any fancy drinks, only booze and water and beer, a few simple mixed drinks, no blender drinks."

These days, there is also no blender in use, but the drinks still get complicated and the names are forever changing, said Lynn Warren.

Two drinks widely known by the locals include the "Salty Dawg" and the "Cowboy Martini." The recipe for the "Salty Dawg" is older than the saloon, said Loree. Made of vodka and grapefruit juice in a salt-rimmed glass, it is a derivative of the well-known "Greyhound."

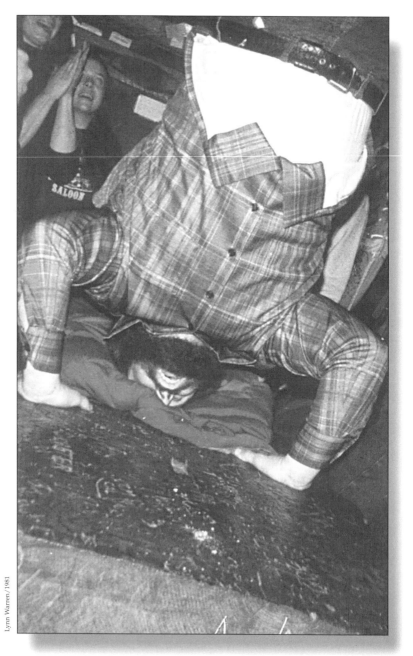

Lynn Warren / 1981

Joe Cavo: "Upside Down and Backwards"

The "Cowboy Martini" — minus vermouth — honors Cowboy, a patron who lived on a sailboat on the Spit. The drink, made of gin, a pinch of salt, and two drops of whiskey, is served with an olive and onion. It was inspired by Cowboy's dad, "a martini drinker from way back."

Throughout the 1980s, the way a drink was served was often more outstanding than the drink itself, according to bartender Diane Svymbersky. One patron would lie prone on the bar and ask the bartenders to pour drinks down his throat. Others liked to drink shots standing on their heads — like fisherman Raven Bailey, who hit the amber light fixture on the ceiling with his feet. "That's why it's broken today," said Diane.

Another version of this game was "Upside Down and Backwards" — a margarita mixed in the mouth while bending backward over the bar. Cissy remembers standing on her head drinking Kamikazes while spotters looked on.

Today, shenanigans like these are met mostly with faded smiles from the bartenders. "The laws have changed a lot," noted Frank Rott, and freedom to indulge customers has been restricted, too.

Employment Agency

Like most fishing pubs in the world, jobs and deals are cemented routinely at the bar. Key marine personnel like Tom VanZanten are pulled from the stools to execute tricky boat maneuvers, repair engines, or round off crews.

At times, Diane Svymbersky has felt more like a personnel agent than a bartender: "The Dawg is a real job finding situation," she said. People call from Bristol Bay, for example, saying "Got any experienced hands around? Send them out!" Notes tacked over the bar contain messages like "Deckhand needed, Float A, Slip 2" or "Thanks for a job well done" — with money for a drink or two pinned inside.

Lynn Warren / 1989

Eric Ringer

The payphone at the Dawg is known to some as "The Office." For awhile, it was the only phone nearby. "It would be tied up for long periods — whether it was a call about a job, or someone sitting there with a roll of quarters talking about a job he or she just came off of," said Lynn Warren.

Hans, who sells exotic sweaters and costume jewelry from Central America on the Spit, uses a credit card and the payphone to conduct business. "I like the atmosphere," he said.

Following the Exxon Valdez oil spill in the 1980s, the pay-phone was buzzing with activity. "People were scared and full of ideas on what should and could be done about the spill," said Lynn Warren. "Our 'office' payphone was ringing off the hook because there were jobs to be had if you fit the right criteria."

Today, employees use the phone (with an unlisted number) behind the bar and the infamous payphone is, as always, still heavily used.

Free Clams

After a good day of clamming across the bay, John and Lynn would steam clams at the bar — an impromptu treat for locals and tourists — melted garlic butter and all.

Hats Behind the Bar

Locals usually know (although some forget) never to wear a hat behind the bar. Getting caught costs money — specifically a round of drinks for everyone. Tourists who don't know about the tradition are quickly warned when they near the "no-hat-behind-the-bar-zone," said Lynn Warren.

Holidays

From the mid-1970s to the late 1980s, elegant Thanksgiving dinners, complete with candlesticks and champagne, were held for anyone alone on the holidays. Loree McGee started the tradition — hosting about 50 hungry patrons, overseeing the turkey basting, and cooking a roast beef. Frank Rott baked beans and supplied another turkey, while fisher-men's wives brought covered dishes.

Lorre McGee/1976

Thanksgiving 1976

Sandy Barker/1993

Mummy Michael Svymbersky and Daddy Joe

After John and Lynn Warren took over, the meals became potluck. The Dawg bought two turkeys and a large ham, and Frank Rott continued to cook his turkey "to perfection" and bake his "wonderful" beans, said Lynn. The Warrens offered a roasted turkey and anything else needed to round off the meal. The turkey carcasses were saved for soup on Superbowl Sunday.

"To some, it was a great surprise when people walked in the door and saw what was going on," said Lynn. "Others made a point of being there and not missing out on all the goodies."

For bartender Cissy Rockett, who came to Alaska in 1982, these occasions were a treat: "When I first came up here, how special it was — especially on Thanksgiving. That was the first time I'd ever been that far away from my family. It was like a family at the Dawg."

Christmas dinner, complete with fresh eggnog and "Mary or Sam" at the piano, was on a smaller scale — but just as plentiful, said Lynn. Diners mostly worked on winter fishing boats far from home.

Each February, the Dawg opened on Frank Rott's birthday. To put the word out, "bushline" messages were sent over KBBI 890, the local public radio station: "Frank's birthday party, same time, same place, come on down." The bash always included homemade cakes, ice cream and games.

On St. Patrick's Day in March, a huge feast is spread for anyone who stops by. "This is one of the best days for us," said Sandy Barker. "It's wonderful seeing locals and tourists come in for a meal, great conversation and green jello. Plus it's the only time I can actually make John help with the cooking!"

When John W. and Lynn lived in Homer, the Dawg provided 30 to 40 pounds of corned beef, 20 heads of cabbage, 15 pounds each of carrots, potatoes and onions — all heated up by John W. and Frank in an old kettle outside. Snow or rainstorms sometimes caused the cooking to move indoors.

Lynn Warren/1985

Frank and Claudia

Lynn Warren/1983

Bringing in the New Year: Cowboy (Center) and Friends

Today, the bar closes down on Halloween and remains closed through Thanksgiving and Christmas. After March, when the bar normally opens again, the locals focus on fishing and the upcoming summer season.

The elegant holiday meals will always be a highlight for customers of the Dawg, said Lynn.

Housecleaning Parties

From the mid-1970s, housecleaning parties helped the owners tidy up after a busy season. "It was a lot of work and fun, and it looked so nice when it was all cleaned and done," said Lynn Warren. A three to four day project, Lynn described how she and John W. did things:

"First we removed all the sawdust from the floors. Then, all the pictures, T-shirts, flags, hats and business cards were taken down and stored. The bar and back area (cash register, coolers, refrigerator, etc.) were covered with large tarps. When everything was protected, John would hose the place down with water from ceiling to floor and out the doors. We would let it dry overnight. The next day, we would take all the washable items to the Laundromat and put fresh paint on the floors and walls. Everything else would get cleaned and dusted before they went back up. Of course, before we opened for the next year, we would fine-tune and dust everything all over again — but the major dust and grime was already removed."

SINK YOUR TEETH INTO THIS

The old man wasn't feeling well. While weathering the waves on a halibut charter off the Barren Islands, the grandpa vomited over the side — dropping his dentures overboard.

He may have lost his choppers, but he kept his sense of humor: "The teeth on the next halibut are mine," he shouted.

But he wasn't so lucky — he spent the rest of his trip to Alaska gumming his food.

OVERHEARD AT THE DAWG

John W. Warren and Peter Udelhoven, Silver Fox Charters

Lights On/Lights Off

"When the lights went on in the tower, we were open; off we were closed. We had a CB radio and some of the fishermen in wintertime would call if it was getting late to say 'Don't close, we are on our way in.'" (Loree McGee)

For many fishermen, the Dawg's beacon light is their "magnet to shore," said Lynn Warren. "It means they are home, they are done fishing. It means 'land.'"

The bartenders, if they aren't completely ready to lock up and head home, have opened the doors and served at least one drink before turning off the light, said Lynn.

Landlubbers, too, look for the beacon to determine if the Dawg is open. When Frank Rott couldn't sleep in his nearby apartment, he would often notice what time the bar closed by following the light. "Who worked last night?" he would ask Lynn; she would tell him. "Oh, she worked hard — the light was on 'til 4 a.m."

Lynn Warren/1987

Diane Wood/1992

Seanda Reid: Ship's Engineer and Dawg Lover

Neckties

"If a fellow happens to wear a necktie at the Dawg, he's likely to get the end cut off," said Lynn Warren. After that, the man usually removes the pieces, unbuttons his top shirt button, and feels more human, she said.

Opening/Closing Dates

At first, the Dawg was open year-round. Under the Hillstrands, a drink could be had from Memorial Day to Labor Day, and bartender Willie Flyum sometimes opened in winter. Under Loree and Bob, the Dawg closed only on Christmas. And again, in the 1980s, the Dawg was open year-round.

In those "always open" days, winter fishing was viable in Kachemak Bay and Cook Inlet, said Lynn. The harbor was alive with activity. About 1984 or 1985, the winter fishing industry slowed down, and little shrimping or crabbing was happening

Sandy Barker/1993

Frank's 86th Birthday

99

in the bay. Because of this, the Dawg started closing in November.

Locals objected to the reduced hours: "Where will we go with the Dawg closed? You can't close the Dawg!" But the Warrens found that closing for a spell each year worked well. It gave the hard-working staff a chance to revitalize, and it cut down on the burn-out factor.

Most recently, the Dawg has opened from Frank Rott's birthday (February 26) to Halloween. With Frank's passing in 1994, those dates might change, said Lynn Warren.

Lynn Warren/1982

Homer Winter Carnival Outhouse Races: Pete Reid Riding and Ken Lipsky Running

Opening/Closing Hours

When the Abbotts had the bar, it was open all night, said Phyllis Abbott. Under the Hillstrands, Frank Rott recalled going in at 5 a.m. to "kick people out." "That was fine," he said, "because in those days, there wasn't a handier place to go to the potty in the morning." More recently, the Warrens have specific seasonal hours.

While the Dawg has remained unlocked later for thirsty seafarers, it has also opened earlier for the arrival of cruise ships, said Lynn Warren:

> "In the early 1980s, when the cruise ships would come to town, they would offload their ship-to-shore boats filled with passengers right below us on the Salty Dawg ramp. A lot of them would come in with their box lunches to sit and visit. Some would have a drink or two, and others would just walk through with their cameras and 'ooh and ah.' They were only in Homer for about four hours."

Outhouse Races

In the early 1980s, patron Ken Lipsky fashioned a lightweight "outhouse" for the Homer Winter Carnival races. Made of fiberglass-coated cardboard and a three-wheel bicycle frame, it was operated by 2 racers with 4 runners sprinting alongside. The event usually started at Alice's Champagne Palace and ended up at the Fire Hall. Diane Svymbersky and Pete Reid rode up front to at least two victories. "It sure was a lot of fun and a great group effort," said Lynn.

ALASKA WOMAN WAYS

Comment of visitor Larry on the easy-goingness of Alaskan women:

"Are you always like this or when you go home do you turn into women?"

❋ ❋ ❋

ALASKA MEN

The supposed "six-to-one" ratio of men to women in Alaska is contradicted locally by the popular saying:

"The odds are good but the goods are odd."

This ratio holds true only in bush communities, noted one woman patron:

"If you can get there by car, so can everybody else."

OVERHEARD AT THE DAWG

Ringing the Bell

Ring the bell by the bar, and it's free drinks for everyone at the expense of the bell ringer.

Round Cards

Bell ringers are awarded a personalized card in memory of the deed. These cards began in the Loree and Bob days.

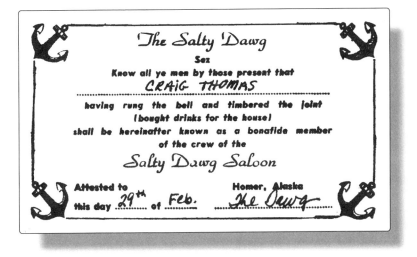

Spider Webs

This is a tradition from the bar's earliest days, although not adhered to anymore: Anyone who broke a spider web on one of the pirate paintings was required to buy a round for the house, according to Florence Jones Elliott, an early Spit cannery worker.

Lynn Warren / 1983

Spit Rat Club Beach Party

Spit Rat Club

In the late 1970s or early 1980s, anyone who survived a winter on the Spit and passed initiation was eligible to join the "Spit Rat Club." Members held membership cards and wore jackets, pins and sweatshirts.

Counting about 25 members, the club developed unique traditions that are still in use today. Presidents (like Frank Rott, Loree McGee and Alex Chapple) pounded on the bar with a special gavel. The Sergeant-at-Arms (like Jim Haigh) pounded on members (not really) with a bat which is still on display at the bar. Designed for fun and camaraderie, the club met once a month and involved "partying, good food and drinks."

Initiation was part of the party, according to Cissy Rockett. Men performed "crab walks" on their backs, while women recited "Peter Piper" or something similar with soda crackers in their mouths. If the women did too well, more crackers were added.

Cowboy's memories were more colorful: Prospective members stood on their heads, and drank a "rat piss" concoction which was "real difficult to get down," he said. One woman, wearing a dress, was minus underwear when it was her turn: "No problem — she got the job done anyway," said Cowboy.

Frank Rott remembered the club's "cuss box," designed to deter bad language — but rarely did: "There was a lot of money in that can, I'll tell you!"

Some of those dollars helped pay for big outdoor parties organized by the club with lots of food, drink and volleyball. "Mary and Rosemary" played the ukulele with Frank, while everyone sang songs around the campfire.

Back at the Dawg, Frank's presidential routine included a 2:00 p.m. visit to his designated "Power Seat" — the first seat at the bar. "If anyone was sitting there, they had to get up. If I was late, people thought I might be sick and they'd come and check on me," he said.

LOREE'S (Award-Winning) HAWAIIAN CHICKEN:

1 broiler-fryer chicken cut in parts
1 tsp. MSG (if desired)
1/4 cup corn oil
1 large onion, sliced
2 cloves garlic, minced
1 can (16 oz.) pineapple chunks, drained and
    syrup reserved
3 Tbls. soy sauce
1 bay leaf
1/2 cup flaked coconut
1-1/4 cup water, divided
1 tsp. chicken base (paste)
2 Tbls. cornstarch
1 cup diagonally cut celery
2 medium tomatoes, peeled, cut into wedges
1 green pepper, seeded, cut into 1-inch strips
1/2 tsp. salt
1/4 cup toasted slivered almonds

Sprinkle chicken with MSG. Heat corn oil in large fry pan over medium heat. Add chicken and brown on all sides. Remove chicken, add onion and garlic. Cook until tender, but not brown. Return chicken to fry pan. Add pineapple syrup, soy sauce, bay leaf, coconut, one cup of water and the chicken base. Mix well. Simmer covered for 20 minutes.

Mix remaining 1/2 cup of water and corn starch. Stir into mixture. Add pineapple chunks, celery, tomatoes, green pepper (which some people like to omit) and salt. Simmer covered, 10 minutes or until fork can be inserted into chicken with ease. Serve over hot cooked rice. Sprinkle with almonds. Makes 4 servings.

People vacated their seats for Frank out of respect, said Lynn. The Club also bought him a chair with a special back to make him more comfortable during his daily visits. Frank favored the Power Seat spot, she said, "because you can see everything going on, it's close to the bathroom, and people can belly up to talk to you."

Before he died, Frank gave his Spit Rat jacket to one of the Hillstrand boys who hocked it for a six-pack of beer — an act totally in tune with the club's spirit, said Frank.

Power Seat

Still in existence today, and named by former bartender Kevin Murphy, the Power Seat was, at first, designated for the president of the Spit Rat Club. For awhile, the seat had a special, leather-tooled seatback which now hangs on the wall.

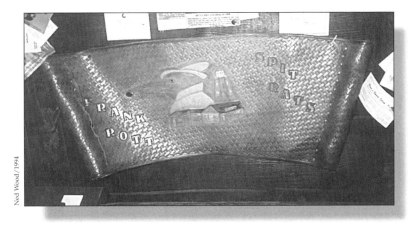

Ned Wood/1994

Recipe

Loree McGee, co-owner of the Dawg from 1974-1980, was a great cook. Her chicken recipe won third place in the 1977 Alaska State Chicken contest, although rumor has it she should have won the main prize.

Weddings

Some patrons feel such an affinity for the Dawg, they choose to hold special occasions there. Countless weddings and receptions have been held over the years, including ones for Cissy and Chuck Rockett, Alex and Ken Lipsky, Katie and Peter Karwowski, Bill Snyder and wife, and "Dave and Anna" — a random list.

Katie and Peter Kawowski

Chuck and Cissy Rockett: 6/13/92

Loree McGee / 1977

Another Wedding Celebration

Loree McGee / 1975

Snyder Wedding

Ned Wood / 1994

Ned Wood / 1994

ARTIFACTS

Every nook at the Dawg is tacked with miscellaneous hanging things. Some of the more outstanding ones are:

Business Cards

Business cards from every place imaginable line the walls and ceilings of the Salty Dawg Saloon. Originally, they were tacked up for practical reasons, but today it is customary to do it as a way of saying "I was here."

Crab

A few mounted crab grace the Dawg's walls as a faint memory of the plentiful crab days. The golden/brown King Crab (with the broken leg) was caught in deep water in 1970 by the BESSIE M near the Barren Islands. Patron Fred Bannick, who reportedly stuck his finger in the crab's pincher and screamed "bloody murder," mounted the unusually colored crab, according to Cowboy.

The mounted tanner crab labelled "F/V KASILOF" and dated "November 1984," is of average size. It honors John W. Warren's boat. But John didn't catch the crab, noted Lynn Warren, it was a gift to the bar.

A lamp with a crab-body shade also hangs in the Dawg.

First Customer/First Dollar

Frank Rott was Loree McGee's first customer: "I had him autograph the dollar bill he paid for his beer with. I kept it, and a large old dollar bill I had for 30 years, with a $20.00 bill from Australia. I put them in a frame and hung it by the cash register, but it disappeared."

Local businessman Willie Flyum was Gerlene Warren's first customer.

Loree McGee/1976

Lana, Loree and Salty Dawg Flag

Lynn Warren/1986

Flag (Salty Dawg)

An oil rig from Kenai, waiting in the inner bay for the weather to clear, was slated to journey to California. The rig's manager said to Loree: "You know, it would be nice if we had a flag of the Salty Dawg to fly on our rig all the way to California."

Loree got busy, made a flag (see photo), and gave it to the man before the rig sailed. The flag made it all the way to California, including under the Golden Gate Bridge. A month later, the man brought the flag back to Loree and she hung it on the ceiling. After that, Loree made more flags and some fishermen flew them over their boats. (See back cover.)

Flowers

A few years ago, Lynn Warren (who has a green thumb) began beautifying the outside of the Dawg with flowers. Now John L. and Diane Svymbersky plant "anything that might grow in the wind and salt," according to Diane.

Heater

While the new heater is not a true "artifact," it holds importance to some colder-blooded patrons.

During a day at the Dawg, the doors open and close a hundred times to admit new customers and to accommodate the thermostats of this person or that. In November 1994, the Dawg got a new heating system and, according to Sandy Barker, "now the winter and fall won't be quite so chilly."

Human Skull

A skull hangs near the cash register reminding customers not to pass bad checks. Legend has it that Earl Hillstrand found it on McDonald Spit 40 or 50 years ago, and put it in his freezer.

Lynn Warren

Ned Wood / 1994

One day, daughter Mo came home from school and noticed something boiling on the stove. Looking in the pot, she couldn't believe what she saw: a skull — in a rolling boil with walnuts.

"What is that?" she asked Earl, who answered: "Oh, it's something I found last summer and I'm going to put it in the Dawg." And since the skull didn't look old enough, he put walnuts in the water to age it.

Life Rings/Wakes

Many orange life ring "wreaths" hang in the bar as memorials to fishermen lost at sea or in other accidents. Some wreaths come from ships or tankers that moor in the bay. A few NOAA rings were donated by crew members who enjoyed the Dawg or who heard about the NOAA benchmarker (see NOAA story at end of chapter).

Along with the wreaths, wakes have been held at the Dawg. One was for Bob Harrison, a fisherman who died when his truck crashed as he was driving to his boat. His parents came to Homer to take him home, and a wreath of flowers was sent to sea in his memory.

George Kapulka was also memorialized by a gathering at the Dawg; his life ring hangs in the poolroom.

In 1994, a special wreath and photograph were mounted to commemorate the passing of Frank Rott.

Money

Pinning cash to the walls started when fishermen left notes with drink money for fishermen on other boats or at sea. While the tradition continues today (mostly with $1 bills or business cards), the amounts used to be larger, said Diane Svymbersky.

Lynn Warren / 1983

Norwegian "Kenny" hands Johnny Lee
a bottle of Scandinavian Liquor

Norwegian *Aquavit* Bottle

In the winter of 1982-1983, the crew of a Norwegian oil rig carrier sailed into Kachemak Bay. In Homer for several months, they became friends and regulars at the Dawg. Some spoke no English, but others translated.

They had so much fun, said Lynn Warren, that they invited a group of regulars to their ship: "They came and got us in their launch boats and treated us with food, drinks and a tour of the ship. All of us Homerites loved the hospitality they showed us."

Before the Norwegians sailed away, Lynn and John invited a group to John's boat, CAPE KASILOF, and gave them care packages and American libations. The Norwegians reciprocated with bottles of a Scandinavian liquor called *Aquavit*. A bottle still hangs on the ceiling today.

After the Norwegians hooked up with the oil rig they were waiting to load, they headed out to sea. "We did receive a postcard from the First Mate when they reached their next destination, Saudi Arabia. Everyone sure missed them when they left. There were some romances that developed and many fond memories of their winter in Homer," said Lynn.

Paintings

The pirate paintings hanging over the bar are copies commissioned by the Abbotts of original artwork that used to hang in the Dawg at its old location.

Shotgun (Double-Barrelled)

This shotgun was brought to the Dawg as a joke for a wedding ceremony. It is owned by Fred Bannick (whose dog "Max" was famous for ringing the bell). The gun hangs above the Power Seat.

Ned Wood/1994

Ned Wood/1994

Spruce Bench

Local Brian Young carved (or, as he would say, "cut") a bench especially for the Salty Dawg Saloon. While most people describe his work as art (he also did the carvings atop Land's End Resort), he remains humble on the point. Located next to the Salty Pup's outer wall (behind the Dawg), the bench is fashioned from local spruce and designed to fit the curve of the back. Almost as weather-weary as the Dawg itself, the bench is a delight to sit on.

Wedding/Divorce/Important Papers

The array is stunning.

Wood Stove

The wood stove sitting outside the Dawg used to be the only heat in the building, said Frank Rott. Loree and Bob also heated by wood stove — one they found outside with "no legs, no grate and a crooked belly." Bob took it to the welding shop and put it back into working order, said Loree:

> "The first year we were open (1974), we had a potbelly stove. The fuel we burned was coal we picked up from the beach. The fishermen would come in cold and wet, take off their jackets and boots, and hang their socks up to dry by the old stove. When the weather warmed, Bob put the stove back outside in the corner of the building and someone stole it."

```
  1        National Geodetic Survey,   Retrieval Date = MAY 14, 1994
UW5498 ************************************************************************
UW5498   DESIGNATION -  HOMER SPIT SALTY DAWG TOWER
UW5498   PID         -  UW5498
UW5498   STATE/COUNTY-  AK/UNDETERMINED
UW5498   USGS QUAD   -  SELDOVIA C-4
UW5498
UW5498   HORZ DATUM  -  NAD 83
UW5498   VERT DATUM  -  N/A
UW5498
UW5498   POSITION    -  59 36 07.06886(N)   151 25 16.94198(W)    ADJUSTED
UW5498   83 minus 27 -      -02.14405            +07.66214        ADJUSTED
UW5498
UW5498   HEIGHT      -
UW5498 ************************************************************************
UW5498   HORZ ORDER  -  THIRD
UW5498
UW5498.The horizontal position was established by classical geodetic methods
UW5498.and adjusted by the National Geodetic Survey in July 1986.
UW5498
UW5498;                      North        East      Scale        Converg.
UW5498;SPC AK 4    -      624,608.261   419,748.650 0.99997891   -1 13 33.8  MT
UW5498;UTM  05     -    6,608,142.973   589,102.226 0.99969730   +1 21 42.1  MT
UW5498
UW5498_THE LANDMARK IS A TOWER
UW5498
UW5498   HISTORY     - Year Condition            Recov. By
UW5498   HISTORY     - 1975 STATION MONUMENTED   NATIONAL GEODETIC SURVEY
UW5498
UW5498                        STATION DESCRIPTION
UW5498
UW5498'DESCRIBED BY NATIONAL GEODETIC SURVEY 1975 (RBM)
UW5498'LOCATED ABOUT 4 MILES SOUTHEAST OF THE TOWN OF HOMER, ON AND ABOUT
UW5498'3/4 MILE WEST-NORTHWEST OF THE SOUTHEAST TIP OF THE HOMER SPIT, ABOUT
UW5498'50 YARDS SOUTHWEST OF THE HOMER SMALL BOAT HARBOR, BETWEEN THE
UW5498'SMALL BOAT HARBOR AND THE PAVED ROAD THAT RUNS THE LENGTH OF THE
UW5498'SPIT AND CONNECTED TO THE SALTY DAWG SALOON.  THE SALOON
UW5498'(TAVERN) IS A LOG HOUSE STRUCTURE.
UW5498'
UW5498'THE STATION IS THE CENTER OF THE TOP OF A WOODEN, LIGHTHOUSE-LIKE
UW5498'TOWER WITH SHINGLE SIDING.
UW5498'
UW5498'A TO REACH DESCRIPTION IS NOT DEEMED NECESSARY AS LITTLE DIFFICULTY
UW5498'IS ANTICIPATED IS LOCATING THE TAVERN AND ITS ADJACENT TOWER.
UW5498'
```

NOAA/1994

Print-Out About the Dawg's Tower Station

THE NOAA STORY

"The Salty Dawg has long been a reference point for seasick sailors in Kachemak Bay. As soon as you can see the familiar lighthouse, you know you're within 20 minutes of solid land, warmth, and a shot of Anisette." (Annabel Lund)

The tallest structure on the Spit, the Dawg's tower, is often used as a landmark by local fishermen. It is also a charted reference point, according to former Commander John Carpenter of the National Oceanic & Atmospheric Administration (NOAA).

In 1975, the tower became a "third-order horizontal position," established by Robert Benjamin Melby (RBM) of the NOAA Pacific Marine Center in Seattle. Horizontal positions are used for determining navigational landmarks similar to fixed Coast Guard navigational aids. Melby, who worked the entire coast of Alaska from Ketchikan to the Aleutians, performed preliminary survey work for the hydrographic ships. "You could always depend on him to do a first class job," said Commander Carpenter. "He was well-liked and respected."

In 1986, the tower's latitude and longitude were readjusted to become more consistent with other worldwide positions:

LATITUDE	59 degrees	36 minutes	7 seconds N
LONGITUDE	151 degrees	25 minutes	17 seconds W

"The Salty Dawg is unique in the sense that it may be the only tavern in Alaska attached to a navigational landmark," said Commander Carpenter. It is located on nautical charts as "Lt.", "Light," or "FLLT/Tower" meaning "flashing light in a tower." (See maps, pp. 12 and 13.)

In a separate action, the crew of the NOAA ship RAINIER installed a commemorative disk on the floor of the Dawg's main building, engraved: "Rainier's Dawg 1978." A year later, the RAINIER's sister ship, FAIRWEATHER, determined the height of the disk (benchmark) and a plaque hangs in the bar with their findings.

At the time, the ships were Seattle-based hydrographic survey vessels operating in Cook Inlet to update nautical charts.

❄ ❄ ❄

Most Dawg owners have noted the friendliness of NOAA crews over the years. Loree McGee keeps a scrapbook of pictures and corresponds with crew members: "The NOAA survey boats were in and out of Homer. They were also our friends and customers. They would invite me over to the ship for lunch and after lunch, I would give each one of the crew a chip for a free drink."

"They've always been a great group of people and so much fun to have visit the Dawg," said Lynn Warren.

122

The FAIRWEATHER

The FAIRWEATHER is named for Mount Fairweather in southeast Alaska. It is 731 feet long, cruises at 14 knots, and carries 12 officers and 57 crew members. It is pictured here at rest in Kachemak Bay. The RAINIER looks so much like its sister ship FAIRWEATHER, "you could hardly tell them apart," said Loree McGee.

I WANNA TAKE YOU HIGHER

With over 13 years guiding fishermen through Alaskan waters, Charter Captain Denny Finlayson often puts halibut-chasing aside for moments of good whale watching.

In the summer of 1993, his close encounter with a humpback near the Barren Islands put the word "whale" on everybody's lips at the Dawg. The animal, weighing about 65 tons (or 10 times the weight of the boat), lifted the charter boat from the water at a 20-degree angle.

The passengers fell to the back.

Forty seconds later, the whale surfaced again, this time pitching the boat to a 45-degree angle.

From the wheelhouse, Denny watched the whale's pectoral fin rise, then crash, into the water. It splashed about 50 gallons of water on board.

That was enough for Denny. He got the boat out of there in a hurry, noticing as he went that the whale was bleeding, possibly nicked by the propeller.

While this was unusual humpback behavior, Denny thought it might have been self-defense. He had seen a pod hovering in the distance; maybe the errant whale was protecting a sick friend. "Or maybe he was just having a bad day."

In spite of the excitement, Denny does not plan to give up his whale-watching anytime soon.

OVERHEARD AT THE DAWG

Chapter 7: STRANGE GOINGS-ON

Exploding Potties

One of the strangest Salty Dawg stories happened in the late 1950s and involved a steel cylinder full of sewage. The story was picked up by newspapers as far away as New York.

In the old days, patrons braved the Alaskan elements to use the outhouse installed by Chuck Abbott behind the bar. ("What else are you going to do?" noted Chuck's wife, Phyllis.) In the unheated single structure, the men's and women's sections were separated by a partition.

When a backup occurred on the men's side, Chuck asked Bruno Agostino, a demolitions expert from the nearby coal mines, for help.

(Meanwhile, two men stopped by the Dawg looking for work, and Chuck turned them away.)

Five feet tall and bowlegged, Bruno dressed in European wool leggings to the knees, according to Mary Gergen, who grew up in Homer. Bruno wore miner's boots, a tri-cornered hat and was experienced with explosives.

"Maybe Bruno could put a little dynamite down there," Chuck told Phyllis, but it was Chuck who actually lit the sticks that day.

In the book "In Those Days," Harold Billups remembered it this way:

> "If one stick would be good, two sticks would be better, so he (Chuck) touched it off. It didn't just blow down as Bruno had said it would. It blew that stench and effluvium around like you couldn't believe. Some of it blew on Chuck's (oil) tanks and on the Salty Dawg. In fact, it pretty well covered the entire end of the Spit."

OVERHEARD AT THE DAWG

BEHAVE, SHE SAID

"I had a machete behind my back, made my husband strip naked, tied him to the bedpost, and beat him with a strap."

"I'd had it," said the lady.

"And then I told him to either get it together or leave."

(Not surprisingly, he left.)

THE GORILLA INDEX

While sitting at the bar, "Don" talked about working for 25 years for a famous department store chain. He started in boy's clothing, he said, but didn't last:

One day at work, a child came in with incredibly long arms. Per his job description, Don pulled some potential shirts off the rack — but all were either too loose in the chest or too short in the arms.

Finally the mother, not focusing on the real problem, blamed Don for not coming up with "just the right thing."

"I thought this store had everything," she shouted.

"Maybe if you try the pet shop," Don countered.

While the store didn't fire Don, they did send him to work in the automotive department — "the dungeon of the operation," he said.

"That's where they sent all their misfits!"

OVERHEARD AT THE DAWG

By some accounts, the raw sewage hit the sides of buildings, a string of laundry, Land's End Resort, a warehouse and a good portion of the end of the Spit.

After putting a "puzzling" sign on the outhouse ("Outhouse Out of Order"), said Phyllis ("How could an outhouse be out of order?"), Chuck went in search of the unemployed men: "I have a job for you..." he told them.

The next day, Phyllis, one of the people who did the follow-up work, noted that "It wasn't pleasant!"

Crab Tales

In the early 1980s, crab fishing was so plentiful that bartender Diane Svymbersky could hardly wait to hear what kind of poundage people got. There was so much crab, she said, that people brought it to the bar and covered the tables and floors with it.

In Loree's day, "Fishermen would bring in 10 or 15 crab and turn them loose on the floor...we cooked them and everyone ate all they could," she said.

Frank Rott remembered the days he couldn't give crab away. "One time I had 13 king crab. I went from camper to camper and asked if they wanted some. 'Is it cleaned?' they wanted to know. It wasn't — so they didn't want it!"

Cissy Rockett

OVERHEARD AT THE DAWG

I CAN'T BELIEVE IT AIN'T BUTTER

Woman at bar: "I just LOVED Last Tango in Paris."

Man: "Well, then. Let's go over to the General Store, pick up a sixpack of 'I Can't Believe It Ain't Butter,' and see what happens."

NOW *THAT'S* PRIVACY

Man to Woman at Bar: "The ceiling of my bedroom is lined with lead. Even God can't see in."

OVERHEARD AT THE DAWG

An Undetonated Bomb

Cowboy talks about a 150-pound World War II bomb supposedly brought to the Dawg in the 1980s. Local Dicky Gregoire pulled it from a crab pot while fishing aboard the VONNIE MARIE in Kamishak Bay.

Immediately, some guys took a hammer to it.

"It could have gone off," Cowboy said with a strange smile.

Treasures in the Dust

At the end of the night, before the lights go out, it is the bartender's job to rake the sawdust floors. While the confusion of spilled drinks, forgotten jackets, and crushed cigarettes creates a disgusting mess to push through, the benefits to the raker can often outweigh the hazards.

Frank Rott searched the dust for fun. "On a windy day, you could throw up the sawdust and watch the coins fall. You'd be surprised at what's there." On one occasion, Frank discovered a diamond ring. He kept the jewel for two years in a little coin purse, not thinking it was worth much. Later, he was surprised when it was appraised at $600.

Mo Hillstrand found "tons of money" and some diamond rings abandoned by couples who would fight, throw their rings on the ground, and shout "I'm not married to you anymore."

Loree McGee has seen people search the floors with metal detectors, but she didn't encourage it. She has also made her share of finds, but the biggest one was ill-fated:

"One night I was closing up and I found $300 under a table. The next morning when I opened the bar, a man was waiting for me. He was so happy that I had found his money."

Viking Brunch at Land's End

Mary and Dave VanZanten

Diane Svymbersky — although never one of the big finders — did find $300 in cash in the dust. And rumor has it that Cissy Rockett has been much luckier, but she won't say what she found.

Although John Hillstrand said "there is no gold in the dust," for one man, the reverse was true:

After dropping a gold tooth on the floor, the man gathered the nearby sawdust into two big garbage bags, emptied them into his bathtub at home, and searched through the muck.

It was worth the effort — he struck gold and retrieved his smile.

Viking Invasion I (The 1980s)

In the early 1980s, the Sunday brunches at Land's End Resort were renowned: "always lots of people, champagne and good food," said Lynn Warren. To add to the festivities, a group of "Homer's finest," including many Dawg regulars and employees, planned a "Viking Invasion" of one of the brunches.

"It was in the planning stage for a short while with everyone connected to it talking about it," said Lynn.

With Homer being a small town, news spread quickly. At the post office, one of the Resort's concerned owners approached John W., hoping to call off the Vikings. John reassured the man that it was all in fun — but no, he couldn't control the Viking Invasion.

Days passed, and the plan proceeded. On the appointed Sunday, everyone met at the Dawg — some dressed in costumes, others with costumes in hand. "The Viking warriors made cardboard horns held to their hats with duct tape," said Lynn. "The Viking maidens just made duct tape horns and taped them in their hair."

Ready for the invasion, the group moved to the harbor and boarded a wooden boat.

OVERHEARD AT THE DAWG

EXPECT ANYTHING

Zooming a camcorder on the locals can be a hazardous affair at the Dawg.

One tourist, after waltzing into the Dawg camera-ready, encountered some bad vibes from a big man at the bar.

Realizing the intrusion, the tourist put his camera aside and tried small talk to ease the tension.

The local was unimpressed and reacted with typical Alaskan directness — he licked the tourist's face.

SORRY I ASKED

Tired of fielding personal questions from strangers, one woman improvised:

"Do you have any kids?" a man asked her.

"Oh, yes, I have five boys — and they're all named after their fathers."

OVERHEARD AT THE DAWG

The seafaring invaders landed on the beach in front of Land's End, while others advanced by foot. "I'm sure the tourists who happened by there loved the show," said Lynn. "The Viking ship skipper threw our waitress over his shoulders and 'kidnapped' her."

After several hours of brunch, champagne and merriment, the group returned to the Dawg. The Vikings stayed in costume, and the maidens removed the horns from their hair: "That duct tape really stuck to their heads. Thank goodness for all the champagne," said Lynn.

Viking Invasion II (The 1990s)

Recently, another Viking event was staged for the 50th birthday of Keith Iverson, author of *Alaska Viking*. Keith is a familiar figure on the Spit, often seen peddling his book to tourists and locals in the summertime.

During Keith's birthday bash, Land's End was again the target of an invasion — this time, an advertised one. The highlight was the Viking ship set afire just offshore — it could be seen for miles.

Later, many attendees stormed the Dawg to continue the celebration.

This was not Keith's first strange experience. He is also famous for being attacked by a bear while hiking in the hills above Sadie Cove. He was carrying two or three copies of *Alaska Viking* in his backpack at the time.

The attack (and personal tumble with a bear) was written up in the tabloids, and caused Keith to miss a New York interview with Walter Cronkite.

This is a true story: the books he carried have pencil-sized claw holes to prove it.

Ned Wood / 1994

Jamming at the Dawg (Note the "Office" phone in the background)

Lynn Warren / 1982

Mary Van Zanten

Chapter 8: *ENTERTAINMENT*

> *"The Dawg has an energy in the heat of the summer season. Even when it is quiet, there is something there. But when it is crawling with tourists and fishermen, there is a buzz."*
> *(An Eloquent Spit Rat)*

For many patrons, fishing village chatter is the greatest form of entertainment at the Dawg. Rolling dice with the bartender for jukebox quarters is also fun — if you win. But when spontaneous music concerts or dancing happens, the enjoyment is so great, everyone is quick to pass the hat.

"Dancing by Expression Only"

Despite the relative quietness of the Spit in the late 1950s, Wilma Williams remembered townspeople "fighting weather" and "hacking ice" to get in to dance at the Dawg. In those days, the jukebox played "Olga the Clamdigger" and "Jorgie Jorgensen."

"Everybody danced with everybody," said Wilma. "You'd be packed in there so tight, you couldn't move your feet." The lack of dance room led to a unique form of "face dancing" — an activity Wilma eloquently dubbed "dancing by expression only."

Ned Wood / 1994

Wilma Williams

Loree McGee

Sax Play

John Child / 1982

Hobo Jim

Musical Murmurings

"It's always been that way," said long-time patron Cowboy about the out-of-tune piano installed by Loree McGee. While some keys are deadened by time and drink spills, Hank Kroll pounded out "amazing" classical piano and Mike Heimbuch played great jazz, Cowboy said.

In the 1970s, Loree recalled jams on the piano, violin and guitar. One patron, an elderly teacher from Soldotna or Kenai, played the piano so well, Bob Sykes playfully ankle-cuffed her feet to the instrument's legs so she wouldn't leave. It worked; she played for hours.

When the bar was half-full and quiet, Loree sometimes distributed sing-along flyers with the words to popular songs. "Everybody would sing and become friendlier with each other," she said.

Hobo Jim, a well-known Alaskan singer-songwriter, partly launched his career singing for screwdrivers at the Dawg. His agent, Suzy Crosby, also a performer, hitchhiked from the Lower 48 to celebrate her 20th birthday at the Dawg (paraphrased):

> First, we shared King Crab on an old fishing boat in the harbor. Then, friends suggested I grab my guitar and head to the Dawg. It was pre-season, a time when many locals are broke and waiting to fish.
>
> When our group walked in the door, someone pulled my guitar out of the case and put it in my hands. As I sang, people filled my guitar case with tips to a 'pretty happy' number. I played until my fingers about fell off, including country, fishing, and original songs.
>
> I have very fond memories of my first time at the Dawg. It was one of the best birthdays I ever had.

Lynn Warren / 1985

Samantha

Lynn Warren / 1982

Peter

Poetry & Song

For better or worse, the Dawg's archives included the following verses. (Since no musical notation accompanied the yellowed pages, patrons are encouraged to make up their own tunes.)

SALTY DAWG CHEER

GIVE A RAH, GIVE A CHEER
FOR THE SAILORS WHO DRINK THE BEER
IN THE POOLROOM AT THE SALTY DAWG SALOON.
THEY ARE BRAVE, THEY ARE BOLD
FOR THE LIQUOR THEY CAN HOLD,
IN THE POOLROOM AT THE SALTY DAWG SALOON.

FOR IT'S GUZZLE, GUZZLE, GUZZLE
AS THEY POUR IT DOWN THEIR MUZZLES
AND AS THEY RAISE A LOUD CHEER
— MORE BEER—

AND IF THE CHIEF OR CAPTAIN SHOULD APPEAR
THEN GIVE THEM BOTH A BEER
AT THE POOLROOM IN THE SALTY DAWG SALOON.

- BARON WOLFGANG VON SULAK

SALTY DAWG FORECAST

Heavy alcoholic haze over all stations
Variable 86 to 100 proof
High scattered whiskey bottles
Lower broken beer bottles
With occasional eggnog
Followed by moderate to strong scotch and soda
Outlook, headaches and bracers
Becoming straight shots by 1200
Otherwise little hope for recovery.
(Forecast valid 12:00 Saturday to 12:00 Sunday)

SUDDENLY, THE BOAT
WAS OUT OF THE WATER - 1964

"It was my turn to be on watch. I think it was about 11 p.m., completely dark, when suddenly the boat was out of the water under both ends. A huge wave had come along and was about to shake the boat to pieces. I cut the throttle. We were on automatic pilot, set for the end of the Spit. The big wave about shook the tar out of that boat.

We got to the Spit just about daylight. There were outhouses and plywood and everything else floatin' around the end of the Spit. We hooked on to whatever we could and brought it in and tied it down to whatever was left in the harbor. We tied boats together so they wouldn't drift...

We heard that the whole Kenai Peninsula had sunk down to the level of the ocean. Of course, we knew that wasn't true because we could still see the Spit. Later we learned that the end of the Spit had gone down at least eight feet and in some places the road was under water."

(Written by Dana & Ruth Newman; used by permission of Ruth Newman.)

PIONEER QUOTES

GOOD FRIDAY EARTHQUAKE

Homer, located in the Pacific's "Ring of Fire," is no stranger to earthquakes. But at 5:36 p.m. on Good Friday, March 27, 1964, a shaker struck with such force, everyone paid attention. Hitting with a Richter magnitude of 8.6 (later upgraded to 9.2), the tremor was followed by 52 principal aftershocks — 11 of them over 6.0. The epicenter, 13 miles below the earth's surface, was located in northern Prince William Sound.

Felt by at least half the population of Alaska, the quake released more than twice the energy of the 1906 San Francisco earthquake. Including oceans, it perceptibly shook over one million square miles.

A tidal wave or tsunami followed, felt from the southern tip of Kodiak Island to Cordova on Prince William Sound. Waves traveled at speeds of over 400 mph in the open ocean, and were recorded on tide gauges in Japan, Hawaii and southern California. The waves finally subsided about 3:55 a.m. the next day.

In Homer, there wasn't a person or a business untouched by the event. People used it as a time marker — "Remember before the big earthquake when...?"

Downtown Homer, about 160 miles northeast of the epicenter, shook violently for over two minutes. The Homer Spit sank 6 feet, but near the Salty Dawg Saloon at its original location, the plunge was closer to 11 feet.

Fractures up to 18 inches wide were seen across the Spit. Eyewitness Glen Sewell reported that one fracture passed between his feet, continued through a building, and crept into Kachemak Bay.

The Dawg Waiting to be Moved Following the Big Earthquake

End of Spit Under Water — April 1964

Within two minutes, by his account, the small boat harbor disappeared into a "funnel-shaped pool." A lighthouse situated on the harbor breakwater reportedly sank 40 to 50 feet. It took nearly $7 million and more than six years to reconstruct the Spit Road.

The Salty Dawg Saloon was empty when the earthquake struck; it was closed that time of year. When it opened soon thereafter, high tides lapped at tire tops and customers' boots, and daily flooding caused high-tide marks on the outside of the buildings.

Historian Janet Klein noted that of the 508 acres on the Spit, 350 were submerged at mean tide. "Before the earthquake," she said, "residents remember the Spit as much higher, drier and wider."

As a result, Owner Earl Hillstrand moved the Dawg to its present site on a plot of land he had owned for years.

Spit Road Under 18 Foot Tide — June 1964

Loree McGee / 1976

A FISH STORY

"Give a man a fish and you will feed him for a day.
Teach him how to fish and he will be gone all season!"

OVERHEARD AT THE DAWG

LAKE STORY

"Fall rains make an island of the famous Salty Dawg Saloon on the Homer Spit" (Headline, "Homer News," Sept. 30, 1976)

Loree McGee was mad as hell and wasn't going to take it anymore. For a while, she kept her sense of humor. She even posed for pictures angling for fake fish in the standing water. But after too many customer complaints, she finally got serious in a letter to town officials and agencies:

"The freshwater lake standing around the Salty Dawg Saloon, the General Store, and fire lanes is constantly being replenished by water from the State Highway drainage ditch and city parking lot.

The winter of '74 and '75, at two different times, we had about 4 inches of water standing inside the Salty Dawg. We bought an expensive pump to pump the water, the hose going across the road (because we do not want to put it into the harbor). The State Highway snowplow ran over the hose and jerked the pump out of the socket, and about that time the power went off for a few hours, so the rest of the night our customers walked around in the water...

John from the General Store has tried for the past few years but has been unable to get help. One needs rubber boots or a skiff to get into either place. My customers who walk into the Salty Dawg tell me about the water and ask where they can park or what I have done to rectify the lake situation around the Dawg...If you are unable to help me, please direct me to a person that can."

— Loree McGee

The outcome, said Loree, was "nothing." The water eventually dried up on its own and disappeared — but not completely.

GENERAL STORE FIRE

*"The Salty Dawg Saloon and the General Store went together like salt and pepper. We sure notice the void."
(Lynn Warren)*

On February 23, 1994, the Dawg's closest neighbor, the General Store (Sportsman Marine Supply) burned in an intense fire. Fuelled by 20-knot winds and more than $1 million in inventory, the fire levelled the store to a parking lot and threatened nearby buildings and vehicles.

The cause may never be determined because of the intensity of the blaze. Flames sometimes reached 50 feet in height.

By the whim of the winds, the buildings that make up the Salty Dawg — some dating back to 1897 — survived.

Over the years, the two businesses shared many customers. A quick source of hot popcorn for Dawg patrons, the General Store carried a large variety of items convenient to the Spit's marine and tourist populations.

Gathering at the General Store

Sandy Barker/1994

Sandy Barker/1994

The General Store Fire

A harbor official woke manager John L. Warren and his fiancee, Sandy Barker, asleep in their nearby apartment. Seeing the intensity of the heat, they called John and Lynn in New Mexico:

"It is so hot, so devastating and in flames," Lynn quoted John as saying. "Just thought I'd let you know."

"Which way is the wind blowing?" Lynn asked.

"The other way," answered John.

"I guess we are saying the right prayers then," she said.

The only damage to the Dawg was melted insulation in a storeroom.

On a breezy fall day in 1994, John noted: "If the wind had been blowing like yesterday, it would have gone for sure."

John Hillstrand feels "pretty bad" about the loss of the General Store: "I liked it out there."

The Fire and the Tower Windows

Lynn Warren/1986

Augustine Eruption - 1986

VOLCANOES

"It hit the Spit at noon. You could see it coming our way, a dark, ominous cloud. It triggered all the outdoor lights to come on and it looked as though it was snowing." (Lynn Warren on the '86 eruption of Augustine Volcano.)

No known active volcanoes exist in Kachemak Bay, but 46 line the Aleutian chain — some along Cook Inlet across from the Kenai Peninsula and in view of Homer.

Augustine Volcano, a cone-shaped island that can be seen from the Salty Dawg Saloon, causes the greatest local concern because of the possibility of tidal waves. It is known to have blown in 1883, 1902, 1935, 1963, 1964 and 1986. When it erupted on March 31, 1986, fallout covered the Spit. It turned a spring day into an ash-covered mess, and caused many locals to stay indoors. Others couldn't sit still: they used panty hose to cover their carburetors so they could drive their cars.

In spite of evacuation warnings issued, at times, every 10 minutes — the Dawg was packed. Some said: "If I'm going to go, I want to go in the Salty Dawg Saloon," said Lynn. Others agreed: "If the Dawg goes — I go."

Lynn Warren/1986

High Noon at the Dawg — Ash Fallout from Augustine 1986

John Child / 1984

The Spit — 1984

The Town of Homer & the Homer Spit

Yukon and Cohen Islands

THE EARLIEST PIONEERS

"They feared evil, and they were energetic, and they always had hope." (Peter Kalifornsky about the Tanainas)

Pacific Eskimos and Tanaina Indians

Artifacts tell us that Yukon Island, not far from the end of the Homer Spit, was once populated by Eskimos. The population vanished, most likely, in the first millennium.

Centuries later, probably between 500 AD and 1785 AD, a group of Athapaskan Indians known as the Tanainas (or Dena'inas) came to Kachemak Bay. The only Athapaskans to inhabit the seacoasts of Alaska, their ancestors crossed the Bering Sea Land Bridge into Alaska sometime before 10,000 BC.

Hunters and gatherers, the Tanaina acquired the skills to thrive in coastal Alaska by learning from their Eskimo neighbors. At the head of Kachemak Bay, on the Homer Spit, and other nearby locations, aboriginal garbage heaps ("middens") attest to the presence of native populations and the local availability of food.

Tanaina Peter Kalifornsky (who died in 1993) noted that the benchlands just above the base of the Spit were a gathering place for hunters before they went to sea.

Traditionally, in groups of small nuclear families, the Tanaina lived and traveled far beyond Cook Inlet and Alaska — as far south as Washington State. According to Janet Klein, "There was a fairly high population of Dena'ina, estimated at two to three thousand people, until the 1830s, when a series of epidemics killed many." Dressed in caribou skins, they lived in matriarchal units and were reported to be taller than their Eskimo neighbors.

ISLAND ARTIFACTS - 1964

"There is no doubt that there has been activity in the Homer area since people first started to migrate eastward from Asia across the ice bridge. Evidence of this has been found on both Elizabeth and Yukon Islands.

In the early spring of 1964, Lou and Eunice Flood were living down on Elizabeth Island. Lou came in with a bucket of water from the little falls that ran down the steep bank into the salty waters of Cook Inlet. When he told Eunice that he had seen a rock that looked too perfectly round and was going back to dig it out, she got her coat and went with him.

Together they loosened the packed dirt around the stone until it fell free in Lou's hand. Quickly he washed it in the stream and gazed in awe at a stone lamp with a figure in the middle. It was their anniversary and turning to Eunice he placed the ancient lamp in her hands saying, 'Happy Anniversary, Honey.'

The Floods...(sent the lamp) to the University of Alaska to have it analyzed and were told that the only others they had known about were found in Manchuria and were felt to be many thousands of years old."

(Used by permission of Wilma Williams & Lawrence Rogers.)

PIONEER QUOTES

The arrival of the Russians ended the Tanaina traditional way of life. Since the Russians did not usually bring women on their expeditions, and often had no hope of returning to Russia, the two peoples intermarried.

From 1838 to 1840, tuberculosis, measles and smallpox spread to the Kenai Peninsula. Survivors fled the rural villages, making the larger town of Kenai the new area native center. Without sufficient resources, many natives became heavily in debt to the canneries. In 1924, natives became eligible to home-stead, but few attempted to "prove up" because of a lack of financial resources.

In 1962, the Indians of the Kenai Peninsula organized an offi-cial tribe. Within five years they filed a protest with the Bureau of Land Management (BLM) against the nearly five million acres of Kenai Peninsula land withdrawn by the federal government. In 1975, the case was settled and Alaskan natives achieved some financial compensation.

❄ ❄ ❄

Today, few, if any, Athapaskans inhabit Kachemak Bay. Disease and the impact of slavery and relocation in the Russian era account for some of this. According to Janet Klein, as of 1981, only about 150 speakers of the Tanaina language remained, and fewer than 10 spoke the Kenai Peninsula dialect.

In the 1990 census of Homer, 113 of 3,600 claimed native her-itage and few claimed Tanaina or Athapaskan/Alutiq heritage. In the nearest Kenai Peninsula towns with native populations, the numbers seem to be growing today.

The Indian phase of Alaskan history lasted nearly 12,000 years.

WHAT'S IN A NAME?

Beluga Lake:
"White Whale" (Russian)

Bishop's Beach:
Named for George & Jane Bishop, owners of Inlet Trading Post, 1955-1976

Diamond Ridge:
A diamond core drill was lost on one of the ridges above town, hence the name.

Fritz Creek:
After "Fritz," the caretaker of the Spit at the turn of the century.

Homer:
For Homer Pennock, a prospector who worked in the Cook Inlet area in 1896.

Kachemak Bay:
Taken from the Aleut word meaning "Smoky Bay," named for the smoldering coal seams in the bluffs.

Ohlson Mountain:
For Henry Ohlson, who lived in Homer from the coal mining days until his death.

(Mostly from "A History of Kachemak Bay:
The Country, the Communities" by Janet Klein)

Homer Facts

Europeans & Russians

In the late 18th century, the Spanish and French launched Alaska expeditions. The British, too, sent envoys, and Captain James Cook charted the coastline looking for the Northwest Passage. He never visited Kachemak Bay.

It was the Russians who made the greatest local impact during this period. In 1786, they established the first permanent white settlement on the Kenai Peninsula at Kasilof — three years before George Washington became president. About the same time, Russian explorers, trappers, fur traders and coal miners settled near Kachemak Bay, seeking to exploit the economic potential of the area.

In 1849, Russian American governor and explorer Mikhail Tebenkov entered Kachemak Bay. His crews built at least one cabin on the Homer Spit and established trading posts on Yukon Island and at Halibut Cove. From these places, furs were gathered, and in particular, sea otter pelts.

Today, about 737 residents of the lower Kenai Peninsula speak Russian at home.

The Russian phase of Alaskan history lasted 126 years.

ALASKA: LOVE IT OR LEAVE IT

"Lilly Walli was a true Alaskan at heart. It was not unusual for her to be a bit curt with a newcomer who was complaining about some aspect of the country.

'How did you get here?' she would ask.
They would reply how and when.

She would reply, 'Follow the same route back then.'"

(Used by permission of Lillian "Blondie" Miller.)

PIONEER QUOTES

Americans

In 1789, the first United States citizens visited Alaska, but they took little interest in the Kachemak Bay area.

In 1867, shortly after the United States took possession of Alaska, the American government sent a survey expedition to establish a military post at Kenai. The survey group, impressed with the Peninsula, reported to Washington that the area was ideal pasture land.

Native people were reportedly not consulted about the sale of Alaska to the United States.

The American phase of Alaskan history continues today. Of the 33,000 Kenai Peninsula borough residents surveyed in the 1990 census, 31,284 speak English at home.

Diane Wood / 1993

THE EXCELSIOR'S ITINERARY

Tuesday, March 10
Homer Pennock's group of goldseekers leaves Denver for Seattle to meet the chartered steam schooner, EXCELSIOR.

Thursday, March 19 - 10 p.m.
EXCELSIOR sails from Seattle for Alaska with 75 men, one woman, and 21 horses aboard. Since Friday sailings were considered bad luck, many men expressed relief when the ship cleared port before midnight.

Thursday, March 26
Boat rounds Cape Ommaney.

Good Friday Morning, March 27
Ship is far up Sitka Sound. Still weak from seasickness, many people go ashore and visit a Russian Orthodox church. For two days, they stay in a hotel while a storm keeps the boat in the harbor.

Monday, March 30
EXCELSIOR finally goes to sea; the storm grows worse.

Thursday Night, April 2
Rounding Cape Elizabeth.

Friday Morning, April 3
EXCELSIOR steams up to the "Homer sandspit" looking for "Fritz," the caretaker.

Saturday, April 10
EXCELSIOR sails south, taking a few malcontents from the Pennock group, and most of the independent gold seekers with her.

Gleaned from: A Game of Bluff (The First of Four Chapters of "Homer's Gold Seekers"), Della Murray Banks, The Alaska Sportsman, October 1945.

Homer History

SETTLING HOMER: THE NEXT WAVE

"There was no smoke, no sign of life at the lone log cabin, and the blast of the steamer's whistle roused no one." (Della Murray Banks)

EXCELSIOR & The Homer Spit

On April 3, 1896, Homer's original 51 sailed into Kachemak Bay. From faraway places and all walks of life, they shared a dream of finding gold, wrote Della Murray Banks — the sole woman on the expedition. Along for the ride were about 25 independent miners, one stowaway, and 21 horses.

From the decks of the steamship EXCELSIOR, the group spied one log cabin, two tumbledown shacks, and the galley of an ill-fated ship at the end of the Spit. Homer Pennock, the group's leader, had chartered the vessel in Seattle and promoted the expedition as a "sure thing." Within a week, all the independent miners and a few group "malcontents" had sailed south.

Those who stayed found the Spit's edges piled with slabs of ice. After cutting a path ashore, they repaired the existing buildings, built a bunkhouse and a headquarters for the Alaska Gold Mining Company. They melted ice for drinking water, and when the season warmed, hauled water from the mainland against difficult sea and weather conditions.

But in a few months, wrote Mrs. Banks, the Spit was alive with violets, "little white stars" and "verdant" green grass.

On October 3, 1896, the still-hopeful group established the first post office on the Homer Spit, naming it after Homer Pennock. This post office remained open until 1907 when mail operations were rerouted through Seldovia.

HOMER PENNOCK: Homer's Namesake

- "He (Homer Pennock) is described as a faultlessly groomed man with irresistible manners, whose occupation has always been separating American millionaires from some of their hard-earned cash."

- "Pennock was more than six feet tall, must have weighed two hundred and fifty pounds, and had a grizzled beard and hair. His gray eyes were hard, keen and shrewd."

- "His genius in crookedness amounted to greatness, it is said, and even after you know this, it is difficult to withhold your confidence and respect."

- "For be it remembered that Pennock always went for big game. The man with a few thousand (dollars) was always safe in his hands."

- "He is ever ready to help a fellow who is down on his luck."

- "Whatever can be said against Mr. Pennock, it is admitted by all that he is no ordinary crook, and I have failed to discover any individual who seemed to harbor the slightest bitterness or ill-will toward him."

- "The last I heard of him he was said to be residing on a beautiful estate on the Rhine, where he could enjoy that quiet and freedom of action that might be to some degree interfered with here."

From "An Adventure in Alaska During the Gold Excitement of 1897-1898," by Bruce Cotten, 1922 (except for the second quote which comes from Della Murray Banks.) Mr. Cotten was yet another citizen separated from his money by the charming Homer Pennock — but he didn't seem to mind much!

Homer History

Those who stayed never realized their dreams of gold, at least in the Kachemak Bay area. By 1897, only nine people still lived on the Spit, mostly in a big log house. The day after Thanksgiving, this house burned down, consuming the group's provisions. "In the end, they all died poor," said Mrs. Banks.

Even the ship had a bitter end: After being remodeled for passenger service, the EXCELSIOR was put to work between Sitka and the Cook Inlet. Later, it was rumored to have gone down in a bad storm with everyone on board.

In spite of the misfortunes, Homer became an official town-site in 1898.

❊ ❊ ❊

In 1900, Cook Inlet Coal Fields Company rejuvenated the Spit temporarily. The Company built an elaborate dock, and the first bit of Alaska railroad. A 42-inch standard gauge, it stretched from the coal mine at Bluff Point on the mainland to the Spit — a distance of about 8 miles.

After the coal was hauled by train to the Spit, it was loaded on ships for the Alaska gold mining towns of Hope and Sunrise — and even to Europe. In 1902, however, the company closed. Mrs. Lillian Walli, an early Homer resident, remembered that, in 1914, the rails were intact and a handcar was still in use by the locals.

❊ ❊ ❊

The first road to the Spit was begun in about 1925. Generally following the route of the old railroad, the construction formed Beluga Lake and still divides the lake from the slough today.

From 1902 until 1914, the town of Homer basically ceased to exist on the Spit. Within a few years, many buildings were torn down to lumber or moved to the mainland. The railroad tracks were removed sometime before 1920.

"I WANT TO GO, TOO": Della Murray Banks

Della Murray Banks — the first woman inhabitant of the town of Homer, Alaska — loved husband Austin and wouldn't travel anywhere without him. In 1896, when he left for a summer of gold-seeking in Alaska, she endured the separation for four days. Finally, she wired him from Denver about her unhappiness.

He missed her, too! In four hours, she packed her things and boarded a train to Seattle to meet him. Twenty-five years would pass before she would see Denver again.

Homer Pennock, the trip's organizer, said that the other wives had wanted to go, too, but Mrs. Banks "just went." He thought she would be put off by the living conditions on the EXCELSIOR, but he was wrong.

Enduring the disapproval of the men, rough seas, primitive sleeping quarters and the general inconveniences of life on the Spit, the 5-foot, 1-inch tall *Denver Times* proof-reader carried her own weight. She scrubbed the beached galley of a ship to make it livable. She voted with the men to name the town of Homer. She explored Kodiak, Cook Inlet and Kachemak Bay by any available means — foot, horse, skiff, steamer or sail — while Austin was off hunting gold. She lost two fingers in a cooking accident. She shot photographs, kept diaries, and like many Homerites before and after her, was mesmerized by the pink summer sunrises over Grewingk Glacier at 3 a.m.

Following more Alaskan adventures, including two trips over the Klondike and the death of her husband, Mrs. Banks settled in Los Angeles. After a disabling fall from a horse in 1923, she spent much of her time writing about the Gold Rush.

On August 29, 1950, she died, survived by her only son, Sydney A. Banks, and three grandsons.

In 1914, fox farms sprang up in the region after local farmers failed at commercial vegetable farming. The animals were descended from wild foxes that an old-timer had captured from a local den. At one point, there were about 15 fox farms and some mink farms. Soon, the problem of finding enough food for the foxes, combined with the low price of fur, ended these ventures.

By 1920, commercial fishing began, and has proved to be the most profitable local business of all. Canneries and about 10 fish-traps between Homer and Stariski Creek thrived. Large schools of herring also brought success to local fishermen.

In the 1930s, most buildings left intact on the Spit were destroyed by a slow-spreading fire. "A few isolated buildings, like the log cabin that later became the Salty Dawg, did escape," wrote historian Janet Klein. The fire was extinguished by the tides over time; there was no rush — the Spit was virtually deserted anyway.

Homesteaders filed claims in the area. And in 1938, work began on modern dock facilities to succeed the old coal dock at the end of the Spit. In the severe winter of 1947, the new dock was destroyed by slow-moving ice. Another dock was commissioned to be built the following year.

With the construction of the Sterling Highway in 1951, and its paving in 1967, Homer was finally linked to the outside world — and a different phase of its history began.

Old Homer Coal Car

Sign on Baycrest Hill

Ned Wood / 1994

Chapter 11: MODERN HOMER

On March 31, 1964 — seven days after the Great Earthquake — Homer was incorporated as a first-class city. From humble beginnings forged by a con-man and 51 miners at the turn of the century, Homer has grown to a population of over 4,000. In the summer, it swells to nearly three times that size.

Roads

Homer is an easily accessible 227-mile drive from Anchorage. But not so long ago, the roads did not exist. In the 1950s, the Alaska Road Commission began the massive project of cutting the Seward/Sterling Highway through the Peninsula wilderness. Before that, pioneers like Clem "Red" Tillion walked hundreds of miles to get where they were going. Even after the highway came, it was perilously unpaved for a few years.

As late as the 1970s, the other main road in Homer — East End Road — was also unpaved. East End Road resident Amy Springer recounted a disastrous, but neighborly tale of the road:

> "I remember how East End Road was 'prepared' for paving late one fall — but left unpaved for the winter. Old-timers shook their heads at the 'expert's' use of culverts in the new roadbed.
>
> That next spring was one of Homer's wettest, and the culverts went tumbling across the landscape and the roadbeds became deep rivers of mud. Road graders buried themselves, and bulldozers were used to pull cars across hastily-filled gullies.
>
> The ingenious pioneer solution: Drive or walk as far as you could, ford the 'creek,' and pick up whatever car waited with keys in the ignition on the other side."

PIONEER WISDOM

That beauty lures many residents and tourists to Kachemak Bay is no secret.

But many pioneer Alaskans, like Martha Wickersham, were a bit more practical about the view:

"Yes, the scenery is beautiful — but you can't eat it!"

(Used by permission of Mary Gerken.)

Homer History

Frank Wood /1993

The Homer Hills

Today, muddy roads still create problems for locals and tourists, even in the summertime. But when the roads are decent, and the fireweed is blazing, driving in Homer is an unforgettable experience.

The View

The view from Baycrest Hill upon entering Homer has prompted many visitors to move to Alaska. (Baycrest Hill harbors the "Halibut Capital of the World" sign.) Expansive views of Cook Inlet's majestic volcanoes are to the north, while the cold, blue-green waters of Kachemak Bay and the Kenai Mountains are straight ahead and to the south. Separating the inner from the outer bay is the Homer Spit — the centerpiece of the town of Homer. From there, many fishermen and women head off to chase halibut, herring, salmon, crab and shrimp.

The order of the Inlet mountains is remembered by locals, from south to north (or left to right), by the acronym "DAIRS" (See map on next page):

"D" Port Douglas
"A" Mount Augustine
"I" Mount Iliamna
"R" Mount Redoubt
"S" Mount Spur

Across Kachemak Bay, Harding Icefield stretches across the glacier-covered Kenai mountains. The largest and most spectacular local glacier is Grewingk, easily seen from many points in Homer, including East End Road.

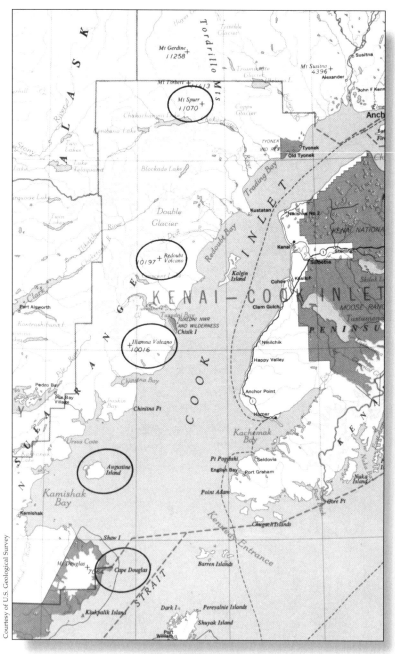

Courtesy of U.S. Geological Survey

"DAIRS" Map

Climate

Sometimes called the "Shangri-La" of Alaska, Homer enjoys the most temperate climate in the state. Temperatures rarely drop below zero, and the lowest recorded temperature is 21 degrees below. The highest was noted at 80 degrees, although it doesn't often go above 70.

The Kenai Mountains protect Homer from severe northern cold while the ocean moderates the northern breeze. Rainfall averages about 25 inches per year.

The two main weather features that cause locals to grumble are overcast summer skies and icy winter roads.

Diane Wood / 1993

John Child

The Homer Spit

Homer Spit

The stretch of land jutting defiantly into Kachemak Bay is the Homer Spit. The "Spit" as the locals call it, is about five miles long and fits its textbook definition — a narrow point of land extending into a body of water. Most likely built by the snout of a retreating glacier, the Spit is made of boulders, rocks and other debris. As layers of sediment were deposited by shoreline currents, the structure grew.

But the Spit is vulnerable. As natural forces build it up, storms and less subtle forces like winds and tides erode it. Old-timers claim that the Spit is a lot smaller today than it was in 1964 before the big earthquake. At that time, the Spit sank nearly 6 feet, buildings and pasture lands flooded, and the small boat harbor disappeared. Gone are picnics under the trees and horses grazing on Spit pastures.

Much of the town's economic and recreational activity centers on the Homer Spit. Aside from numerous businesses like restaurants, fishing charter companies and gift shops, there is a huge, wheelchair-accessible fishing hole. Anyone can step from a car, throw a line in the water — and with luck — hook or snag a king, silver or pink salmon at the right time of year.

Loree McGee/1976

Man with Fish

Ned Wood / 1994

Ned Wood / 1994

SOME UNIQUE HOMERITES

Author, spokesperson and radio personality Tom (End of the Road/"We'll leave the light on for you") Bodett might be the most famous of Homerites (get to know his work and see why) — but a few lesser-known locals are also of interest.

The Eagle Lady

From mid-November to mid-April, Jean Keene — "The Eagle Lady" — feeds nearly 300 eagles daily outside her trailer on the Spit. The "Eagle Spot" is located close to the original site of the Salty Dawg Saloon. Birds fly there to feed from as far away as Kodiak, and as close as the woods across the bay.

Each year, Jean scatters nearly 7,000 pounds of fish heads and cannery scraps to help the birds survive winter's harshest months.

Early in the morning, Jean hauls the fish (mostly obtained from nearby Seward Fisheries) to her trailer area, cuts the load into pieces, positions herself behind a fence, and tosses it out by hand. Viewers are invited to watch, but Jean keeps a close eye on the area. She wants birds like "Henry" (who is easy to spot because he is missing a leg) to remain wild, but protected.

Salmon and octopus are the birds' most favored fare, but most scraps are halibut, flounder or candlefish.

Born in Aitkin, Minnesota, Jean is still spry in her early seventies. Sporting mounds of red-tinged hair, she drives a great big truck around town and works at the local cannery. A hardy soul, she has endured sub-zero temperatures, 70-mile an hour winds, and tidal waves in her windy abode by the sea.

Helen Jackson/1959

Helen and R.B. Jackson at Venta, Alaska

Barefooters

While Homer's unique community blend and abundant churches may be apparent to visitors — the historical groups like "The Fountain" or "The Barefooters," may not be as well-known.

In 1948, after the performance of a Christmas pageant in California, Fountain group members vowed to abandon shoes, let their hair grow and dress in cotton robes until world peace was achieved. In 1956, a spin-off group came to Alaska to homestead land and establish the WKFL (Wisdom, Knowledge, Faith and Love) Fount of Alaska. They left behind a heroic reputation of disaster assistance in California.

By the summer of 1957, the Fountain established a headquarters building, a machine shop, and a community called "Venta" at the head of Kachemak Bay. The Brothers joined the Homer Volunteer Fire Department and Sisters helped form the Auxiliary. Throughout this time, they continued to walk barefoot through the seasons.

In December 1958, at the group's headquarters in California, two former members were asked to leave because of "antisocial behavior." In retaliation, they demanded to see Krishna Venta, the group's leader. Request denied, they detonated 20 sticks of dynamite at the front door, blowing up themselves, Krishna Venta, and nine other people. Aside from revenge, they had wanted to prove that Venta was mortal.

Within a few years, the Alaska Fount slowly dissolved. By 1969, most members had returned to their previous homes in the Lower 48. A few from the Alaskan Fount and California Fountain joined Reverend Jim Jones in the jungles of Guyana in 1978 and, unfortunately, died there.

Helen Jackson/1960

Asaiah Bates and R.B. Jackson at Venta, Alaska

Today, some of the original members continue to live in Homer, including Asaiah Bates, Helen Jackson ("Sister Neria"), and R.B. Jackson. Asaiah is a public figure dedicated to the tenets of the WKFL Fountain of the World. The WKFL Park, located at the corner of Heath Street and Pioneer Avenue, is a "Monument to Peace" and was donated by Asaiah to the town. It is open year-round for the public to enjoy.

Asaiah — his hair still uncut but his feet now sheathed — publishes frequent letters to the editor in local newspapers, maintains a presence at many town meetings and attends every church in town. He is known for his spontaneous kindnesses and for dubbing Homer "the cosmic hamlet by the sea."

The Jacksons have raised their children and live in a house that is a museum of Homer progress since 1957. Helen Jackson is currently sorting through her files and artifacts to preserve them for future community reference. R.B. Jackson copes with the challenges of each day with an infectious sense of humor and an ever-present twinkle in his eye.

Another original member — Jonathan Terry — also still lives in Homer.

John Child

Kondraty Fefelov

Old Believers

In the late 1960s, Russian-speaking women in silken peasant dresses, and bearded men in embroidered shirts, appeared on the docks, streets and at the markets of south Peninsula towns. They came to Alaska to avoid religious persecution and to establish the first Old Believer village at Nikolaevsk near Anchor Point. Later, other Old Believer communities sprang up at the head of Kachemak Bay.

Today, while there are at least a half-dozen Old Believer villages in Alaska, the lives of these people remain a mystery to many locals and tourists.

A deeply religious, non-conformist offshoot of the Russian Orthodox Church, the Old Believers have been on the move for 300 years. At that time, they left Russia to practice their religion in peace, settling on almost every continent in the world, including the countries of China, Australia, and Brazil.

In 1963, they secured voluntary passage to the United States and Canada with the help of the Tolstoy Foundation — and with the personal intervention of U.S. Attorney General Robert F. Kennedy. They established communities in New York, New Jersey and Woodburn, Oregon — a community which continues to prosper, with a population of about 6,000 today.

In 1968, six extended families of the sect headed north to Alaska and the Kenai Peninsula. In 1990, the population of the village of Nikolaevsk numbered about 500, or about 80 nuclear families, with many families counting 8 to 10 children in their ranks.

Other smaller Old Believer villages developed, including Kachemak Selo at the head of Kachemak Bay, to be near water and better farming land. Today, many Old Believer families own boats and work in the commercial fishing industry.

MORE ON THE OLD BELIEVERS

- One main distinction between Old Believer groups is those who recognize priests and those who do not.

- Most families speak Russian at home, although few were born in Russia.

- Men tend to cut their hair and leave their beards untrimmed; unmarried women plait their hair in single braids; married women bind their hair in two braids under a cap called a *shashmura* covered with a kerchief.

- Marriage is encouraged for boys around the age of 17; for girls, as young as 13. Weddings can last three days.

- Many do not purchase food (except sugar and salt) or traditional clothes outside of their community. Many do not accept food from outsiders or allow outsiders to use their dishes or cutlery. Their home brew is *braga*, made from berries.

- Old Believers tend to accept some modern technology, although it is rumored that televisions, when owned, are often kept in closets away from the community eye.

- Religious services begin at 2:00 a.m. on Sunday and last six or eight hours, although the Easter service can last 15 hours. Most members, young and old, stand through all religious services. The church requires roughly 200 fasting days each year and village schools adjust schedules for the numerous religious holidays.

Homer Facts

Kondraty Fefelov and the Old Believer Bible

Inside the Russian Orthodox (Old Believer)
Church in Nikolaevsk Village

Frank Wood / 1993

Appendix

John Child / 1907

By all accounts, the Spit was quiet by 1907 — but some activity must have persisted if this photograph is dated correctly.

John Childs

End of Spit, Turn-of-Century

Part 1: HOMER TIME LINES (1890s-1990s)

HOMER TIME LINE: 1890s-1920s

1896: Homer Pennock and a crew of 51-plus arrived at end of Homer Spit on the EXCELSIOR; first post office opened on Homer Spit.

1902: Town of Homer ceased to exist on Spit because of decline in coal market; Spit stayed relatively dormant until 1915.

1904: U.S. Geological Survey noted 20 Spit buildings still standing.

1907: Spit post office closed; mail rerouted to Seldovia.

1916: Coal industry reopened to fuel homes, canneries and passing steamships.

1919: First school operational.

1922: Kachemak Bay was center of fox farming in Southcentral Alaska for next 10 years.

1923: From the sea, Homer looked wide open, covered with tall grasses and patches of small trees. There were 10 houses and no modern conveniences (except for an old-fashioned telephone system strung over poles and trees.)

1924: First mail flight by Carl Ben Eielson.

1925: First road begun in town.

FOX FARMING AT HEAD OF BAY
(1930)

"The first year in the [silver] fox farming business was quite profitable, giving the fox farmers a very optimistic outlook.

The second year they had many more foxes and were in a position to make a good payday when the Depression hit. The bottom dropped out of the prices and they did not make enough to pay for the medication used in raising them...All along the shores of Kachemak Bay the fox farmers felt the crunch."

(Used by permission of Steve & Lorna Zawistowski.)

PIONEER QUOTES

HOMER TIME LINE: 1930s

1930: U.S. Census showed population as 35; slow moving fire in the 1930s destroyed most buildings on Spit. The fire was extinguished naturally by high tides.

1935: Homer Cash Store opened — complete with oil stove to sit around and a place upstairs to dance on Saturday nights; first "inside" bathroom fixture came to town.

1936: Big influx of new residents settled mostly in hills; many later left for construction and Armed Forces jobs.

1938: Fox farming ventures waned and eventually died because of the Depression and low fur prices; town had two general stores, two restaurants and a hotel.

1939: Shells, coal and driftwood covered local beaches; 13th motor vehicle arrived to stay; 175 homestead families in town.

MAY THE ROAD RISE TO MEET YOU
(1949)

About the Sterling Highway:

"It was at Wayne Jones' camp when the skinners began to hear the sounds of the road equipment working from the Soldotna end. The excitement built each day as we waited for the two crews to meet and forge the final link to the outside world.

We all cheered when that day came in the summer of '49."

(Excerpt from Wilma Williams' book, If You've Got It To Do...Get On With It. Used by permission.)

HOMER TIME LINE: 1940s

1940: Homer Heights School was completed (attended by eight students and one teacher); soldiers in uniforms and big green Army trucks were seen around town for the next decade; population estimated at 325.

1941: Airport opened; boats and ships came to town via Beluga Slough with entrance on front beach.

1943: A room at Bunnell Hotel cost $3 for two; population about 300.

1944: Pink salmon sold to canneries for 7 cents a fish — chums, 9 cents; highway to Homer was reportedly a "mess" from Seward turnoff; concrete footings were poured for Homer's first theater.

1945: Still no roads to Homer; population estimated at 300.

1946: Population 500, 46 children in schools, 28 miles of unpaved road, 7 cars, an airfield large enough for small planes, daily mail delivery, two grocery stores, several churches, a cafe and a lumber yard; Homer's first bar, "The Yah Shure," opened; construction began on Sterling Highway.

1947: A mass of ice moved from the inner bay around end of Spit taking the town dock with it.

1949: The Homer road crew, working northward on Sterling Highway, heard equipment coming from the Soldotna side; 4 students graduated from Homer High School.

John Child / 1956

1st Homer Winter Carnival Beauty Pageant

John Child / 1957

John Child Gathering Coal on the Beach

HOMER TIME LINE: 1950s

1950: Sterling Bar opened — first bar with inside restrooms; first commercial bakery came to town; population estimated at 307.

1951: Sterling Highway was completed, but not paved yet.

1954: Uminski's Department Store started selling furniture and clothing; Homer Volunteer Fire Department used a Jeep pulling a 300-gallon tank on a trailer and a 6x6 truck equipped with an 800-gallon tank to fight fires; television came to Alaska; population estimated at 716; eight churches and 61 businesses in town.

1955: Homer Society of Natural History organized.

1956: Homer Winter Carnival began and included a beauty pageant; first hospital saw patients; Homer Family Theater began showing films around Christmas (Admission: 35 cents/kids, 50 cents/students, 90 cents/adults.)

1957: The Salty Dawg Saloon threw open its doors to thirsty locals; Homer still a rustic, dusty town; Artic (sic) House of Beauty was established and stayed around for 30 years.

1958: Anchorage began house-to-house mail delivery.

1959: Sterling Highway was paved; Homer Roller Rink burned down; Alaska became a state.

WILMA'S EARTHQUAKE STORY

The Family Cafe,
Downtown Homer
March 24, 1964

"Martha's teenage daughter, Margaret, was waiting tables for her mom. She put a milkshake on the mixer. Suddenly, there was a deep, roaring sound that increased in intensity as the easy atmosphere of the cafe tensed. The lights went out and we looked at each other questioningly.

'Margaret, what are you doing with that milkshake machine?' Martha shouted from the kitchen.

Margaret shrugged, bewildered.

Someone shouted 'Ride 'em Cowboy.'

I thought about Tam and Terrill (my children) a mile away. I ran to the road and could see them struggling toward home. As I hurried toward them, a new wave of tremors rolled beneath our feet. They sat on the road, trying to hang on, scared to death.

They saw me coming and got to their feet again.

When I looked into their frightened faces, we took a minute to hug before hurrying homeward.

"We have sure got a mess to clean up at home." I said.

(Excerpt from Wilma Williams' book, If You've Got It To Do...Get On With It. Used by permission.)

Homer History

HOMER TIME LINE: 1960s-1970s

1960: Population estimated at 1,247.

1963: Large road crews worked to finish highway from Anchor Point to Homer.

1964: Homer incorporated as a city (March 31); big earthquake hit March 27.

1968: Old Believers came to town; Pratt Museum opened to public.

1971: Homer's first local Cadillac arrived — GOLD!; water lines were extended to the Spit.

1976: Locals enjoyed drinking Shirley Temples at the Salty Dawg and throwing peanut shells on the floor.

1978: Median age of residents 27.5; 53 percent males; residents averaged 13.1 years of schooling.

1979: Public and commercial radio came to town.

1961

197

Lynn Warren

Liz McBride and Friends

HOMER TIME LINE: 1980s-1990s

1980: Estimated population 2,209.

1983: The Salty Dawg wins the Winter Carnival outhouse race.

1985: New post office built; Pioneer Avenue paved; McDonald's came to town.

1986: New high school built; Mount Augustine blew, turning day into night at high noon.

1987: Winter fishing in Kachemak Bay is almost non-existent.

1989: The great Mount Redoubt eruption (December); Eagle Quality Center came to town.

1990: Population 4,300 year-round residents; average resident 30 years old; Homer featured in McDonald commercials during Superbowl XXIV.

1994: General Store burned down on Spit; locals marooned on Spit for a few hours during a huge, destructive storm.

1995: The Salty Dawg Saloon opened as usual on Frank Rott's birthday.

Lynn Warren / 1987

*Weekend at the Dawg: Diane Svymbersky (Left)
and Tom VanZanten (Right)*

Jane Pascall / 1992

Kiwi Ian Carpenter, a Frequent Seasonal Visitor to the Dawg

Part 2: GLOSSARY

Around the Corner

The farthest area across the Bay to the right you can see from the Spit or Baycrest Hill. *See Pogi.*

Break-Up

Start of spring.

Cheechako (v. Sourdough)

Newcomer to Alaska versus someone who has survived many Alaskan winters.

Homerite

Person residing in Homer, Alaska.

Meat Hunters

People fishing to stock their freezers rather than for sport.

Middens

Aboriginal garbage heaps.

Openers

Periods of time (usually short and intense) designated by the U.S. Department of Fish & Game when fishermen can fish for certain types of fish. New laws might make openers obsolete.

Outsider

Anyone not living in Alaska.

Going Outside

Leaving Alaska, especially for the Lower 48.

Packboard

A kind of backpack for supplies used in the early days in Homer.

Parking Lot

Kisses stolen outside in the Dawg's perimeter.

"Pogi"

Standing at the front of the Dawg and looking toward Cook Inlet, Point Pogibshi is the last bit of land you can see in the distance. "Pogibshi" is Russian for "perilous." *See Around the Corner.*

Power Seat

The first seat on the short side of the bar. Used to be reserved for Frank Rott, once president of the Spit Rat Club, every day at 2:00 p.m.

Prove Up

To fulfill the legal requirements and prep work to own a homestead.

Pukers

Tourists who can't keep their breakfasts down when fishing on the water; also the boats they are on.

Scenic Overload

Something tourists sometimes experience even after a short visit to Alaska. Akin to "cathedral overload" in European cities.

Sixpack

A type of charter fishing boat that is designed to carry six people.

Sixpacking

Treating someone to a drink six times at once.

Slimers

Someone who works with fish guts on a line at a cannery.

Spit Rat

A person, often college age, who lives in a tent on the Spit. Spit Rats usually work at the local canneries or on local fishing vessels and have very little access to standard conveniences like showers. They are usually the biggest tippers at the Dawg, according to Cissy.

Wannigan

A kind of trailer lived in, for example, by families building the Sterling Highway.

PART 3: BIBLIOGRAPHY

BOOKS

Alaska Historical Commission. Who's Who in Alaskan Politics. Compiled by Evangeline Atwood and Robert N. DeArmond. Alaska: 1974.

Alaska Pioneers of the Lower Peninsula. In Those Days. Homer: Alaska Pioneers of the Lower Peninsula, 1991.

Alaska, University of. Anthropological Papers of the University of Alaska. Vol. 23, Nos. 1-2. Fairbanks: 1991.

Cotten, Bruce. An Adventure in Alaska: During the Gold Excitement of 1897-1898, A Personal Experience. Baltimore: Sun Printing Office, 1922.

Dolitsky, Alexander. Change, Stability, and Values in the World of Culture: A Case from Russian Old Believers in Alaska. Alaska: Alaska Dept. of Community and Regional Affairs, 1991.

Grantz, Plafker & Kachadoorian. Alaska's Good Friday Earthquake, March 27, 1964, Geological Survey Circular 491, A Preliminary Geologic Evaluation. Washington, D.C.: U.S.Dept. of Interior, 1964.

Klein, Janet. A History of Kachemak Bay, the Country, The Communities. Homer, Alaska: Homer Society of Natural History, 1981.

Klein, Janet R. and Donna L. Lane. Historic Homer: A Building Survey and Inventory, Phase I.

Naske, Claus-M. and Herman E. Slotnick. A History of the 49th State. Michigan: Wm. B. Erdmans Publishing Co., 1979.

Pedersen, Walt and Elsa. A Larger History of the Kenai Peninsula. Sterling: Adams Press (Chicago), 1983.

Williams, Wilma. If You've Got It To Do...Get On With It. Anchorage: Alaska Press, 1995.

ARTICLES/PERIODICALS

Alaska Magazine. (April 1974): 71.

Alaska Magazine. (June 1980): 64.

Banks, Della Murray. Alaska Sportsman. "A Game of Bluff." Vo. XI, NO. 10 (October 1945): 10.

Banks, Della Murray. Alaska Sportsman. "Prospecting Trip to Kodiak." Vol. XI, No. 11 (November 1945): 18.

Banks, Della Murray. Alaska Sportsman. "Inside and Out." Vol. XI, No. 12 (December 1945): 14.

Banks, Della Murray. Alaska Sportsman. "Hope Springs Eternal." Vol. XII, No. 1 (January 1946): 14.

Carlson, Phyllis D. "Homer — An Historical Vignette."

Cline, Steve. "The Constant is Change." (Publication name and date unknown).

Cole, Marjorie K. Fairbanks Daily News. "Native Tales Translated in Dena'ina Legacy." (March 22, 1992).

Elko, Andrew E. Alaska Magazine. "The Eagle Lady of Homer." (September 1982): A17-A20.

Gay, Joel. Alaska Magazine. "Old Believers in a Time of Change." (October 1988).

Godwin, Connie. Anchorage Times. "Top Chicken Cooks To Vie for Crown Saturday." (May 12, 1977).

Herman, Anne L. Alaska Magazine. "Jean Keene: Homer's Eagle Lady." (October 1989): 80.

Huber, Frank. New Alaska Outdoorsman. "The Eagles' Spot: Jean Keene, the Eagle Lady." Vol. 2. No. 2. (1992): 52-53.

Lund, Annabel. Homer News. "Between the Lines." (February 3, 1966) and (September 28, 1978).

Reynolds, Christopher. Los Angeles Times. "Homer, Alaska: They Left the Light On." (August 7, 1994): L-1.

Smith, Giselle. "End of the Road." Alaska Airlines Magazine, (August 1990).

Somers, Randi. Homer Tribune. "Original Spit Rat Dies at 87." (May 24, 1994).

Off Duty: Diane and Joe Svymbersky

PERSONAL INTERVIEWS

Phyllis Abbott

Sandy Barker

John Carpenter

Tim Carr

Cowboy

Suzy Crosby

Florence Jones Elliott

Mary Gerken

John Hillstrand

Mary Margaret "Mo"
Hillstrand

Helen Jackson

Christ Jacober

Janet Klein

Loree McGee

Lillian "Blondie" Miller

Richard Minton

Bruce Olmstead

Jane Pascall

Cissy Rockett

Frank Rott

Amy Springer

Diane Svymbersky

Tom VanZanten

John L. Warren

Lynn Warren

Sherri Wilkins

Wilma Williams

O.N. Schemanski

PHOTO/ILLUSTRATION/MAP CREDITS:

Phyllis Abbott

Sandy Barker/John L. Warren

John Child

Mary Margaret Hillstrand

Steve Hillyer/Art Unlimited

Helen Jackson

Loree McGee

Richard Minton, NOAA

Jane Pascall

Cissy Rockett

Olivia Schemanski

Diane Svymbersky

U.S. Geological Survey

Lynn Warren/John W. Warren

Edmund "Ned" Wood

Frank Wood

GENERAL HELP:

Everyone quoted in the text, plus:

A.T. Publishing & Printing

Joy Griffin

Homer Library

Homer Public Library

Deborah Jamieson

Kinko's Copies

Lousaac Library, Anchorage

Paul Martone

Richard Minton, NOAA

Pratt Museum, Homer

Amy Springer

Time Frame

U.S. Geological Survey

Sherri Wilkins

Frank Wood/Raquel Wood

Ned Wood / 1993

Cove Across the Bay (Seldovia)

Part 4: INDEX

SELECTED INDEX

213

SALTY DAWG SALOON SOUVENIRS

Salty Dawg T-shirts, sweatshirts, and other souvenirs
are available directly from the Salty Dawg Saloon,
P.O. Box 2581, Homer, Alaska 99603.

Ned Wood / 1994

Loree McGee

A HISTORY OF KACHEMAK BAY: THE COUNTRY, THE COMMUNITIES

by Janet Klein

Available in Homer from the Homer Society of Natural History, Eagle Quality Center, The Bookstore or by mail from:

PRATT MUSEUM
3779 Bartlett Street • Homer, Alaska 99603 • (907) 235-8635

$7.95 (Plus $1.50/book first class postage and handling)

IN THOSE DAYS
Alaska Pioneers of the Lower Kenai Peninsula
(The Book)

Exciting true stories and historic photographs of homesteading, fishing, establishing businesses, fur farming, mining, and public service back "In Those Days" on the Lower Kenai Peninsula. Published by the Pioneers of Alaska, Igloo 32, Auxiliary 14, Homer, Alaska.

Order Form

Name: _____

Address: _____

Zip: _____ Phone: _____

Please send the following books:

# OF BOOKS	TITLE	PRICE	TOTAL
	IN THOSE DAYS (This is a high-spirited, high-quality hardbound book, 8-1/2"x 11", with numerous photographs, a blue and gold foil cover, and over 200 beautiful pages. Makes a wonderful gift for anyone interested in the early days of Alaska.)		$27.50

Mail orders to:

Pioneers of Alaska Book Fund
IN THOSE DAYS Book Committee
c/o P.O. Box 2549 • Homer, Alaska 99603.

The book is also available at local bookstores in Homer, Alaska.

ART BY STEVE HILLYER

To order an 11"x17" ($25) reproduction suitable for framing of the print of the Salty Dawg Saloon and General Store in Chapter 9, please write the following address:

Steve Hillyer
Art Unlimited
P.O. Box 664
Prineville, Oregon 97754

KIANA BED AND BREAKFAST
Homer, Alaska

In Homer, join hostess Amy Springer for old-fashioned
Alaskan hospitality, warm comfortable rooms, and an
expansive view of Kachemak Bay and Grewingk
Glacier.

Diane Wood/1994

Amy Springer
Kiana Bed & Breakfast
P.O. Box 855
Homer, Alaska 99603
(907) 235-8824

Diane Ford Wood

Diane enjoyed the best whale stories of her life at the Salty Dawg Saloon. Before coming to Alaska, she graduated from New York University and worked as a newspaper reporter in Peterborough, New Hampshire. She busked, babysat, and cooked her way around the world — spending three months cooking on a Queensland, Australia cattle station.

In Homer, she hosted *Sense of Place*, a weekly volunteer radio show on KBBI Homer Public Radio. She also worked as a legal secretary.

Diane is married to Edmund "Ned" Wood and, at age 42, became a first-time mother with the arrival of daughter Andie Siobhan Wood in 1994.

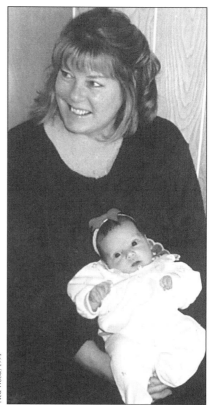

Ned Wood / 1994

FROM ALASKA PRESS:

Alaska Landmark Series:

THE DAWG'S TALE
by Diane Ford Wood
The Story of the Salty Dawg Saloon,
The Homer Spit
& The Town of Homer, Alaska

❄ ❄ ❄

Alaska Pioneer Series:

HOME SWEET HOMESTEAD
by Joy Griffin
Sketches of Pioneer Life in Interior Alaska

THIS IS COFFEE POINT, GO AHEAD
by Wilma Williams
A Mother & Her Children Fish Bristol Bay, Alaska

IF YOU'VE GOT IT TO DO...
GET ON WITH IT
by Wilma Williams
One Family's Life in Early Homer, Alaska

ORDER FORM

Please send the following books:

# OF BOOKS	TITLES	PRICE	TOTAL
	The Dawg's Tale	$15.95	
	Home Sweet Homestead	$15.95	
	This is Coffee Point, Go Ahead	$15.95	
	If You've Got It To Do...Get On With It	$15.95	
	Postage/Handling ($2/book, $.50 each add'l book)		
	TOTAL:		

Name: _____

Address: _____

Zip: _____ Phone: _____

Mail orders to:
ALASKA PRESS
P.O. Box 90565
Anchorage, AK 99509-0565

Thank you for supporting the efforts of ALASKA PRESS to pre-serve the memoirs of early Alaskans and the histories of Alaskan landmarks. In return, we would like to personalize your book. Please include inscription information with your order and allow 4 weeks for delivery.